THE COMPLETE GUIDE TO ENGLISH BULLDOGS

David Anderson

LP Media Inc. Publishing

www.lpmedia.org

Publication Data

David Anderson

The Complete Guide to English Bulldogs ---- First edition.

Summary: "Successfully raising a English Bulldog dog from puppy to old age" --- Provided by publisher.

ISBN: 978-1-07082-816-9

[1. English Bulldogs --- Non-Fiction] I. Title.

Design by Sorin Rădulescu

First paperback edition, 2019

Cover Photo Courtesy of Shayla Brown

TABLE OF CONTENTS

INTRODUCTION **8**

CHAPTER 1
A Unique Look – The Bulldog **10**
The Face And Physique Of A Fighter – But They Are Really Lovers . . **11**
Wrinkles Are Apt For Their Wisdom **13**
About The Colors... . . . . **15**
About That Short Snout... . . . . **15**
Friendly, Loyal, And Entertaining **17**

CHAPTER 2
Breed History And Characteristics **18**
A Contentious History **19**
   Three Theories Of Their Heritage **19**
   A Tough Job **21**
Personification Of Love And Loyalty **23**
Drooling And Flatulence – Be Prepared **23**
Mascot Of Choice **24**
English Versus American **25**

CHAPTER 3
The Ideal Home **26**
Best Environment **27**
   A Great Dog For Almost Every Home **27**
   Even No Yard Is Fine – They Aren't High Energy **28**
   A Great Watchdog **28**
   Floor Surfaces **28**
   Nearly Perfect Family Pet, But Be Careful Of Heat And Cold **29**
Ideal Lifestyle **30**
   Strengths **30**
   Intelligent – Plan To Train Them **31**
   Loving Loungers **32**
They Go Where You Go **33**

CHAPTER 4

Finding Your Bulldog **34**

Adopting From A Breeder **35**

    Finding A Breeder **35**

    Health Tests And Certifications **39**

    Contracts And Guarantees **41**

    Puppy Genetics – The Parents **42**

    Selecting Your Puppy **42**

Adopting An Older Dog **44**

    Benefits **44**

    Rescues **44**

    Warning About Socialization **45**

    Introduction To Children And Other Pets **45**

CHAPTER 5

Preparing For Your Puppy **46**

Preparing Your Kids **47**

Preparing Your Current Dogs **50**

Dangerous Foods **53**

Hazards To Fix **54**

    Kitchen And Eating Areas **55**

    Bathroom And Laundry **56**

    Other Rooms **57**

    Garage **58**

    Outdoors And Fencing **58**

Supplies And Tools To Purchase And Prepare **61**

Planning The First Year's Budget **62**

Keep Things Out Of Reach **62**

The Puppy Area **63**

CHAPTER 6

The First Week **64**

Preparation And Planning **65**

The Ride Home **67**

Digestive Issues **68**

First Night Frights **68**

First Vet Visit **71**

The Start Of Training **72**

    The Leash **72**

    Teaching Respect **73**

    Consistency **73**

    Acclimation To The Home **73**

CHAPTER 7

The First Month **74**
Not Up To Full Strength **75**
Setting The Rules And Sticking To Them **76**
Early Socialization **77**
Treats And Rewards Vs. Punishments **78**
Exercise – They Don't Need Much **80**
Best Activities **81**
Beware Of Heat, Be Careful Of The Cold **81**

CHAPTER 8

Housetraining **82**
Understanding Your Dog **83**
Key Words **84**
Inside Or Outside **85**
They Are Intelligent – But You Still Need To Be Consistent **86**
Positive Reinforcement – It's About Respect . . . **87**
Regular Schedule, Doggy Door, Or Newspaper . . **87**
It's All On You – Bulldogs Have The Brains, You Bring The Patience . **89**

CHAPTER 9

Socialization And Experience **90**
Benefits Of Socialization **91**
   It's Easy **91**
   Problems Arising From Lack Of Socialization . . **91**
   Why Genetics Matter **93**
   Predictable Pet When Properly Socialized . . . **93**
Common Problems **93**
Properly Greeting New People **95**
Behavior Around Other Dogs **95**

CHAPTER 10

Being A Puppy Parent **96**
Staying Consistently Firm **97**
Possible Problems With Bulldogs And Managing Behavior **99**
Managing Gnawing And Chewing **99**
Playtime! **101**

CHAPTER 11

Living With Other Dogs **102**
Introducing Your New Puppy **103**

Working Dog Mentality **106**
Biting, Fighting, And Puppy Anger Management **107**
Raising Multiple Puppies At Once **108**

CHAPTER 12
Training Your Bulldog Puppy **110**
A Gentle, Consistent Approach **111**
Gain Their Respect Early **113**
Operant Conditioning Basics **113**
Primary Reinforcements **114**
Secondary Reinforcements **114**
Why Food Is A Bad Reinforcement Tool **115**
Small Steps To Success **116**
Why Trainers Aren't Always Necessary, But You May Want One **117**

CHAPTER 13
Basic Commands **118**
Why Their Personality Makes Them Ideal Companions **119**
Picking The Right Reward **119**
Successful Training **120**
Basic Commands **121**
    Sit **122**
    Down **123**
    Stay **123**
    Come **124**
    Leash The Puppy **124**
    Leave It **124**
Where To Go From Here **125**

CHAPTER 14
Nutrition **126**
Why A Healthy Diet Is Important **127**
Commercial Food **128**
Preparing Your Food Naturally At Home **128**
Puppy Food Vs. People Food **129**
Dieting, Exercise, And Obesity **130**
Warning About Overfeeding And The Right Caloric Requirement . . . **131**

CHAPTER 15
Grooming – Productive Bonding **132**
Managing Your Bulldog's Coat – It's Easy **133**

Puppy **133**
Adulthood **134**
Skin Care **135**
Trimming The Nails **137**
Brushing Their Teeth **137**
Cleaning Their Ears And Eyes **137**

CHAPTER 16
Health Issues **138**
Fleas And Ticks **139**
Worms And Parasites **141**
Benefits Of Veterinarians **143**
Holistic Alternatives **144**
Vaccinating Your Bulldog **145**

CHAPTER 17
Health Concerns **146**
A Dog With A Lot Of Possible Health Concerns **147**
Face **147**
Body **148**
Typical Pure-Breed Health Issues **148**
Where You Can Go Wrong **148**
Importance Of Breeder To Ensuring Health In Your Bulldog **149**
Common Diseases And Conditions **150**
Prevention & Monitoring **151**

CHAPTER 18
Your Aging Bulldog **152**
Senior Dog Care **153**
Nutrition **154**
Exercise **155**
Mental Stimulation **157**
Regular Vet Exams **157**
Common Old-Age Ailments **159**
Enjoying The Final Years **159**
Steps And Ramps **160**
Enjoy The Advantages **161**
What To Expect **161**

INTRODUCTION

When you see an English Bulldog, there is never any question about the breed. Absolutely no other dog looks anything like a Bulldog (although a few other breeds do have some similarities). With their bowed legs, low-hanging jowls, and fierce underbite, English Bulldogs look rather fearsome. However, their curly tail is a much better indicator of what this breed is actually like. Fun-loving, loyal lap dogs (or at least so they think), Bulldogs are practically the embodiment of what you want in a dog.

Their looks and fierce-sounding bark come with a number of advantages. Bulldogs make for great guard dogs because many people don't realize just how affable and caring these dogs actually are. With its intimidating demeanor, this breed has become one of the world's favorite mascots. From school rallies to sports events, saying "Go Bulldogs!" will quickly win you favor in many places around the world. The fact that Bulldogs are actually incredibly friendly canines is what makes them so wonderful as a mascot too. You can take them to games, and they will represent your team with humor and affability that you won't find in many breeds of dogs.

As a well-established breed, they do have some serious health concerns. The biggest potential risk is overheating. Bulldogs absolutely need to be in the air conditioning, particularly in the summer during the heat of the day. They don't require much exercise, which is fortunate considering the fact that they cannot handle heat. They also do not do well in the cold, particularly as puppies.

Bulldogs are surprisingly intelligent dogs, but they can come with quite the stubborn streak. As long as you are firm and consistent with your approach, they can learn remarkably quickly. They are frequently at the top of the class in obedience schools and can even join competitions to show off their surprising agility. Of course, if you prefer just to lounge around the home, that is perfectly fine with them. Bulldogs can be a source of nearly constant entertainment because they really just want to be with their family, and they can't help but make you laugh. They are great for nearly any family too.

Bulldogs are fairly easy to groom. They shed at a low to moderate rate, and their short hair does not require more than about weekly brushing. The primary concern with Bulldogs is the folds of their wrinkles; these need to be cleaned regularly to keep the wrinkles from becoming dirty or infected.

Both loyal and loving, Bulldogs are great family pets. They make good travel companions or lounging buddies. It will not take most English Bulldogs long to become a part of the family.

Photo Courtesy of
Michelle Naumovski
IG @Mayortysonbulldog

CHAPTER 1
A Unique Look – The Bulldog

Nearly every part of an English Bulldog gives away its breed. From that unmistakable face to the curly little tail, when you see a Bulldog you know that it is a Bulldog. They have a distinctive walk, and you can usually hear a Bulldog coming because of their short snouts and the resulting loud breathing.

Despite looking like the toughest dog on the block, Bulldogs are an amazingly sweet, entertaining, and loving dog that can easily change the way you perceive them.

Chanda Barnes of Barnes English Bulldogs perfectly sums up the most notable features of Bulldogs: "The flat squishy face, undershot jaw, the rope across the top of nose, Cinnabon tail and short legs." These are all of the features that you are likely to notice, and they are all a part of the Bulldog charm.

The Face And Physique Of A Fighter – But They Are Really Lovers

"Bulldogs love any and everyone. They can be very comical. Not a day goes by without one of them doing something that will make me laugh."

Kym Thew
Bullyful Bulldogs

What most people notice first about Bulldogs is their incredibly distinctive face. If someone were to point out a Bulldog's face, one of the first things that may come to mind is a mugshot. This is a breed that looks like they are tough and ready to fight at any given moment. However, that look is not even close to the personality of most Bulldogs. It is more of a reminder of where they came from than what they are like today.

The Bulldog's small snout is emphasized by an underbite that often makes their lower teeth jut out over their upper lips. As if this weren't obvious enough, their jowls hang down over the sides of the lower jaw, as if to highlight their unique face. Their eyes are accented by wrinkles that make them look like old souls staring out at you from the floor.

English Bulldogs are not particularly tall, but they have a very stout physique. You can see a bit of their history in their bowed legs (they once worked with bulls and were much fiercer than they are today). Because they have such an unmistakable gait, you can tell by the very sturdy-looking body that a Bulldog is fairly durable and tough. Most weigh between 40 and 60 pounds, though they are not nearly as tall as most other breeds in their weight range.

The finishing touch to this very distinctive breed is the usually spiraled tail. It certainly seems out of place, a small odd touch on this otherwise intimidating-looking dog. It is probably the best indicator of what the dog is like – surprisingly adorable.

FUN FACT
Bulldog Club of America

The Bulldog Club of America (BCA) was formed by a group of English expatriates in America in 1890. It became incorporated in New York State on November 29, 1904. The BCA now operates across the United States and is an officially recognized breed club by the American Kennel Club.

Photo Courtesy of
@emmitt_the_Bulldog on Instagram

Wrinkles Are Apt For Their Wisdom

The wrinkles on a Bulldog's face are one of their most distinctive traits and part of what makes them so endearing. Those wrinkles are actually very appropriate on the Bulldog, just like the tail. Despite their tough appearance, Bulldogs are a fairly intelligent dog. It was necessary in their past for them to be able to work with much larger bulls. The brains of a Bulldog are much keener than most people realize.

Photo Courtesy of Brenda Bishop

Instead of looking at the sturdy frame of the Bulldog, consider those wrinkles. They are the indicator of the brains behind that unique face. Bulldogs are a wise breed because they learned how to work, and then realized that it is much better to hang out with the family. The experiences of previous generations have taught them not to sweat the small things and to simply enjoy what their family has to offer. They can be quick to make you laugh and can be incredibly patient with children.

The wrinkles are important beyond just the wisdom that they hint at though. They are typically deep enough to require regular cleaning to ensure that the skin under the wrinkles does not get infected. Cleaning the wrinkles is well worth it because your Bulldog will enjoy the fact that you are giving him or her more attention – even if she doesn't entirely enjoy the washing part.

Photo Courtesy of
Christopher Liley

About The Colors...

At first glance, Bulldogs do appear to come in a very wide range of colors. However, this is often an indication that they were mixed with other breeds to provide a "unique color" for the dogs.

Bulldogs typically come in the following colors and patterns:

- Brindle (striped)
- Solid white
- Solid red
- Fawn or fallow
- Patches of different colors over a white or fawn color

If you find a Bulldog that does not come in the traditional colors (particularly if that is the breeder's primary selling point), you will want to ask a lot of questions about the dog's heritage. Kym Thew of Bullyful Bulldogs has warned about the dangers of choosing a Bulldog when the colors are the main focus of the breeder.

There is no such thing as a "mini" Bulldog; Bulldogs that are blue, tri-color, merle, etc., are not purebred Bulldogs. They were crossed with some other breed somewhere in the lineage to get these so-called "rare" colors.

The coat itself is going to be fairly easy to manage. Bulldog fur is short and glossy, so it does not require a lot of brushing to keep the shedding down. They are not hypo-allergenic though, and Bulldogs do shed.

About That Short Snout...

The incredibly distinctive snout of the Bulldog – wide and flat – actually contributes to a couple of the breed's issues. Bulldogs are part of the brachycephalic canine breeds, which means that they are one of the few dogs that have both a short head and a short nose.

The one fact that most people do not know is that it is difficult for Bulldogs to breathe when they need to cool down. The labored breathing can sound cute, but that is why you have to be very careful of your Bulldog. They have trouble getting rid of heat by panting like most dogs. This means that it is incredibly easy for them to overheat. If you are the kind of person who prefers to huddle in the air conditioning in the summer, you will find your Bulldog is a like-minded creature that will be far more comfortable sitting by your side.

*Photo Courtesy of
Karlye Kennedy*

Because they have trouble cooling off, they are not a dog that is good for jogging with.

The flat nose can also contribute to problems with your Bulldog's eyes and teeth, too. You will want to always take good care of the wrinkles, and while you are cleaning the wrinkles, monitor the rest of the face to make sure your dog is healthy. Ask your vet about the things to look for to make sure you catch any potential problems early.

Friendly, Loyal, And Entertaining

Bulldogs look distinctive, but it is their amazing personalities that really make this breed so popular. They are incredibly patient, and many of them will put up with young children with the same patience that you do. The life expectancy of a Bulldog is far too short at 8 to 12 years, but the dog's popularity is a testament to just how much people really love the breed.

They are incredibly loyal and will protect you if needed, but for the most part they are a very relaxed and friendly breed that mostly just wants to enjoy life. Believing themselves to be lapdogs, they are going to want to put your legs to sleep to be close to you or to sit in your lap. They will stay pretty close to you, hanging around for whatever attention you will give them and to make you smile when you need it most. Just being around Bulldogs can be enough to make you feel much better about your day.

CHAPTER 2
Breed History And Characteristics

The English Bulldog's appearance is rooted in the history of the breed. While historians and naturalists argue about the heritage of the Bulldog, their history as a working dog is far easier to understand. This is a breed that had a very difficult job in the early days, and their appearance reflects that rough and tumble work. Over time though, the Bulldog came to be much more than just a capable worker – the breed learned how to simply enjoy living.

They are fiercely loyal, but often are very gentle about their loyalty. If you want a loving dog that will greet you at the door and be ready for some hugs and play, you would be hard pressed to find a more affectionate pup. Bulldogs are every bit as loving as Labs and Golden Retrievers, just with a much shorter, stockier frame.

Photo Courtesy of
Pierre Messier

Photo Courtesy of
Heather Granger

A Contentious History

If you want to start a heated debate among people interested in Bull-dog genetics, simply ask about the heritage of the Bulldog. You will quickly find that the origins of the species is far less well-known than its history as an active part the workforce.

Once you learn about what Bulldogs used to do, you will wonder how they managed to survive. That incredibly stocky frame and distinctive gait make a lot of sense when you know why it would evolve to look so rough and solid.

Three Theories Of Their Heritage

The first theory is that the Bulldog preceded the Mastiff. Given how big Mastiffs can be, this can be hard to envision.

The second theory is that Bulldogs are the result of breeding Pugs and Mastiffs. This idea does seem more likely at first glance as the Bulldog shares some qualities of both of these breeds. Their faces also resemble that of the Pug, though their noses do protrude more than the average Pug's face.

The third theory is that the Bulldog descended, along with the Mastiff, from the Alaunt (now extinct). This was a large dog that was typically used

Photo Courtesy of
Robert Williams
Tallmadge Photography Studio

by butchers to manage oxen. The Alaunt would intimidate the oxen into staying in their stalls. This seems fairly plausible as it shows how Bulldogs and Mastiffs had the same heritage, evolving differently based on the work they would do. Considering that the term "Mastiff" was used more generically until the last century or so to indicate any bulky or large dog, this theory seems to be the most likely.

Whatever the origins of the Bulldog, they ended up being quite the interesting breed.

There is possibly a reference to them as early as 1576 AD in one of the earliest versions of books about dogs. This book did not mention Bulldogs by name, but did reference a unique-looking (the term "ugly" was used) dog that when paired with another of its kind could manage an untamed bull. Before that, the term "Bandog" was used for many different types of dogs, but the mention of a particular broadmouth British dog used to fight appeared in Roman texts. The Romans were so intrigued that they sent some back to Rome. While this certainly was not the Bulldog of today, it is very likely an ancestor.

A Tough Job

One of the reasons Bulldogs tend to be intelligent is that they were working dogs. And they had one of the hardest jobs you can ask a dog to do.

Photo Courtesy of
Gail Deeble

Prior to becoming a pet, Bulldogs worked to manage bulls, a creature far larger than they were. The short, stocky frame made it much easier for the dog to deal with something so much larger. Sometimes they served as guard dogs for bulls; other times their role was to bait or control the bull. During this time, people believed that a bull that was baited before being killed would taste better and would provide more nutrition. If a bull was not baited first, the meat was considered unfit to be eaten. It was also a sport that the nobles and those of means enjoyed watching.

The first time the Bulldog was referred to specifically was in this context. In a letter from one English noble to another in 1631, the Mastiff and Bulldog are mentioned separately, showing that they were no longer considered to be the same breed.

Given the work they had to do, the singular appearance of the Bulldog makes sense. Looks were not the point of the dog in the early days; as long as the dog could hold its own against a bull it was accepted. As people realized that bull baiting was not only pointless but wrong, Bulldogs transitioned into other work. Some were bred with Terriers (particularly Bull Terriers) to make other breeds because Bulldogs actually did not make great fighters. They may be able to take on a bull, but they aren't adept at fighting other canines.

When bull baiting was banned (1802) and the law finally enforced (1835), Bulldogs became less popular. They enjoyed some renewed interest during the Victorian era when people took an interest in strange-looking dogs, and they have never really dropped out of the public consciousness since then.

Despite their incredibly intimidating appearance, people found that the Bulldog was actually an amazing companion. And if there is any breed that uses its looks to its advantage, it is the Bulldog.

Photo Courtesy of
Jonathan Nickel

Personification Of Love And Loyalty

"Bulldogs have an impressively strong appearance and sour mug that could easily intimidate any man, however, they are quite loving and affectionate and will be quite content with simply relaxing on the couch with you."

Melissa Riley
Stone Quarry Bulldogs

Bulldogs definitely look fierce, and anyone who sees them without having met one before is understandably scared at the sight of such a distinctive-looking canine. However, Melissa Riley of Stone Quarry Bulldogs put it best when summing up their appearance compared to their personality: "Bulldogs have an impressively strong appearance and sour mug that could easily intimidate any man, however, they are quite loving and affectionate and will be quite content with simply relaxing on the couch with you."

Bulldogs love their families more than nearly anything else, and they will become like a noisy, bulky shadow that follows you around the house. They don't complain, though they will sometimes give you a disapproving look if you are doing something to annoy them. They may be intelligent enough not to be anybody's fool, but for you and their family they are more than happy to be a fool if it makes you happy.

Drooling And Flatulence – Be Prepared

If there are two things that you should know before deciding to get a Bulldog, it is that they are prolific droolers, and often they are rather flatulent as well. With a wide lower jaw and such pronounced jowls, drooling should be a foregone conclusion. However, they also tend to be quite gassy as well, thanking you for the meal with a bout of belching and farting.

They are well worth the effort of owning as a pet, but know that you will have wet spots around the water bowl more often than not. And quiet nights on the couch will be accented with a few noises that don't come from the TV.

Photo Courtesy of
Leah Paley

Mascot Of Choice

Bulldogs are the favorite mascot of schools, and quite a few sports teams use them as well. Given their incredibly tough look, this makes sense in terms of wanting to scare a rival team.

However, it is the personality of the Bulldog that really makes them a fantastic choice as a pet. They are intelligent, loving, and entertaining, which makes them great with crowds. When properly trained, Bulldogs can be incredibly entertaining, doing tricks and generally having fun with the people around them. According to Kym Thew of Bullyful Bulldogs, "They can be very comical. Not a day does not go by that not one of them [her Bulldogs] will do something that will make me laugh." With this kind of desire to entertain, they are great for working crowds at sporting events.

English Versus American

There are a few differences between English and American Bulldogs, and they tend to be very easy to spot.

When you think of a Bulldog, you probably imagine the English Bulldog. They are short and stocky with an expression that seems to be a constant glower. The English Bulldog is a descendent of the bull baiters in England, and tends to be between 40 and 60 pounds. They aren't meant for lots of exercise and they are quiet pets. The American Kennel Club allows you to register an English Bulldog as it is a breed with an established history.

HELPFUL TIP
Drool Bibs

Bulldogs are known for their propensity to drool, but that doesn't mean that their drooling needs to make a mess. Consider purchasing a dog drool bib for your pup to help eliminate the mess. Drool bibs for dogs are available in many online pet shops or can be a fun DIY project!

American Bulldogs definitely have the look of the Bulldog, but they are a good bit taller and heavier. With a much wider healthy weight range (70 to 125), they can be a full head or more taller than their English counterparts. Their faces can look like a mix between a Bulldog and a Pit Bull. They are far more athletic and can be noisier as well. There is no registration for American Bulldogs with the American Kennel Club. They also require a much firmer handler than the English Bulldog.

CHAPTER 3
The Ideal Home

Bulldogs have such a great personality and such a gentle disposition that they are perfect for almost every home. They are remarkably patient with kids, and can be very protective of them. When you do go out for your regular walks in the early morning or evening, you are going to find that people gravitate to your Bulldog, and your Bulldog will love the extra attention.

Falling squarely into the category of a medium-sized dog, they do not require nearly as much space as other dogs in this classification. Mostly they are interested in being near you, whatever it is that you happen to be doing. Since lounging is one of their favorite pastimes, Bulldogs don't require much indoor space. With their extreme intolerance of heat and susceptibility to extreme cold, they aren't going to want to be outside for long periods of time most of the year. Some indoor playtime or a short bout outside is enough for these dogs.

Photo Courtesy of
Deborah Egler

Best Environment

Those stern faces hide a very affable and gregarious disposition. Bulldogs are notoriously easygoing, and can put up with a lot of annoyance from their family members (as long as they are properly socialized). They can live on a farm or in a one-bedroom apartment and be perfectly content either way. If you like to travel, your Bulldog just wants to go with you.

Photo Courtesy of Brian & Brandi Kozlowski

Bulldogs aren't demanding, but are more than happy to entertain others. They love to be in a crowd or at home alone with you. There are not many breeds that are as easygoing as the Bulldog, which is what has made them such a popular pet in many different homes.

A Great Dog For Almost Every Home

Bulldogs are surprisingly quiet dogs, which is good when you consider that their voices are loud when they feel the need to be vocal. Since they don't require a lot of exercise, they are good in almost every home, even an apartment.

With a passion for life and a charisma that often makes them the center of attention, they can find a comfortable role in most homes. However, you will need to be aware of the temperature inside and outside to keep your dog healthy. They can overheat very easily, and don't tend to do particularly well in the cold. When it gets hot outside, you will need to be able to run the air conditioning to keep your furry baby cool. In the cold of winter, make sure that there are warm places for your puppy or older Bulldog to lie down.

For puppies, you will need a fairly sizable space for the puppy to remain when no one is around. Having a medium-sized crate will also give them some space of their own even after they don't need a puppy area.

Even No Yard Is Fine – They Aren't High Energy

Photo Courtesy of Jayden Perks

A couple of short walks every day is about all the exercise Bulldogs need. If you have a yard, they will be more than happy to play with you in it (not on a hot or particularly warm day) or just lounge around with you.

Most of them are not great swimmers, so they aren't going to want to spend time in a pool or playing in water. They also should have sunscreen applied before going out on sunny days (in the early morning or evening). With all of this care, it is a good thing that they don't require a yard.

A Great Watchdog

Bulldogs may be loving, affectionate, easygoing dogs, but they can be very protective of their people too. They have earned their reputation for being dangerous to those who mean their family harm. As the bulldog is a relatively quiet breed, you might think they aren't as effective as a dog that does bark, but that does not mean they won't go to check out the source of unexpected noises.

Probably the best defense with a Bulldog, though, is their appearance. There are not many people who look at a Bulldog and don't feel some level of apprehension if they don't know the dog. That stern mug and bulky frame are one of the best deterrents that you could ask for in a dog – that and the fact that they are not going to go around barking at every little sound.

Floor Surfaces

The Bulldog may have a sturdy frame, but all you have to do is watch a Bulldog walk to see that they have an interesting challenge. You will want to keep your pooch from slipping on slick surfaces or hardwood. Slippery floors, such as laminate and hardwood, are dangerous to all dogs, but particularly to those who tend to mess about, do tricks, and generally play most of the time. Bulldogs are not an exception when they get excited and want to play with you. Keep your Bulldog from sliding around by either putting non-slip rugs on the floor or add special mats that are made to stay in place. This will protect your furry companion, as well as keeping your family a little safer.

Nearly Perfect Family Pet, But Be Careful Of Heat And Cold

"Most people think that Bulldogs are aggressive, they are not. Bulldogs are great with children. Many people do not know that a Bulldog cannot go on jogs with you or stay outside in hot weather for long periods of time. Bulldogs are not outside pets. They should be kept indoors in a temperature controlled environment."

Benjamin De Jesus
www.championbullies.com

There are two things that it is nearly impossible to overemphasize.

1. Bulldogs are fantastic family pets.

2. Bulldogs overheat very easily, and it can be fatal.

The Bulldog's natural disposition is incredibly friendly, contrary to the expression permanently on their faces. They have a tendency to want to be friendly, unless their family is threatened. It is remarkable how such a stout, grizzled-looking dog can be so patient and gentle with children who think the Bulldog is a big toy. Of course, you will always need to be present when your young children are around the Bulldog, but Bulldogs today are not typically aggressive or vicious.

With the way their faces are structured, Bulldogs are not able to regulate the heat of their bodies like most other dogs. They may drool an astonishing amount, but it is not nearly as effective at cooling them down as other dogs with longer muzzles.

They are an indoor dog and should never be left outside. If you live in a warmer climate, you will need to schedule walks around the coolest parts of the day, and the walks will probably still need to be short to en-

HELPFUL TIP
Don't Let Snow Slow You Down

Dog lovers who live in colder regions or who enjoy staying active during the colder months know that it's important to make sure their dogs are properly equipped to deal with harsher climates. Coats and boots are not just good for keeping people warm, they're also a great way to keep your dog comfortable. Make sure to do your research and choose correctly sized shoes and coats for your dog's comfort. And remember to be patient; your dog will most likely need some time and training to become used to wearing these accessories.

sure your dog doesn't overheat. As pointed out by Sandra Fulton-Cooper of Bodanna Bulldogs when she was asked about a Bulldog's exercise needs, "Short walks on cool mornings or evenings. Never leave them outside unattended to prevent overheating/death." It is a sad truth, but Bulldogs simply cannot handle heat, and they are one of the most likely breeds to suffer heat stroke.

Always be aware of the conditions outside and inside to make sure your Bulldog is comfortable.

Ideal Lifestyle

Some Bulldogs very much enjoy being fairly active. They can compete in different types of courses, and they can often be found at the top of the class in obedience school. Many of them are couch potatoes. A fair number of them can be influenced by small dogs, and will believe that they, too, are a lap dog. If you allow your Bulldog on the couch, you will probably want to make it clear that their place is beside you, not on top of you.

With their primary focus being on family, they don't mind traveling either. Given how intimidated people will likely be if you travel with a Bulldog, it is like having your own little bodyguard, right down to the bouncer physique and intelligent stare they can give people.

You can also feel comfortable bringing a Bulldog puppy into your home with children of all ages and other pets. If they don't have a preconceived notion of other animals or kids, their default mode is to love everyone and everything. Rescuing a Bulldog is a bit more of a challenge as their personal history will paint how they view other animals and kids. This aspect will be covered in more detail in the next chapter.

Strengths

Almost everything about the Bulldog's personality could be considered a strength. They are loyal to a fault, and they attract attention like you would not believe for a dog that has been unkindly referred to as ugly. However, that is part of their charm. After staring someone down, your Bulldog will open that massive mouth and start panting, as if to break the ice with strangers. Once that personality starts to show through, it is difficult to see them as intimidating.

Their intelligence means that they can help to entertain you on hot days when you want to stay close to the air conditioning. If it makes you laugh, all the better.

When young children want to play with them, Bulldogs will sit down and absorb the attention. If the kids get a little rough or a little loud, your Bulldog will give you a look as if to say, "Please make them stop." Then he will wait for you to intercede. A well-trained Bulldog will put up with a lot more than most dogs.

Because of the way they look, people who don't know better think that Bulldogs are aggressive or vicious. This is one reason they are a great addition to the family. Just having a Bulldog can be enough to dissuade others from trying to break into your home. If someone does, your Bulldog will not take it lying down. They are incredibly protective of their people against perceived threats. With their history of taking on bulls, they are formidable protectors.

Photo Courtesy of Jo Wormald

Intelligent – Plan To Train Them

Baiting bulls may not have encouraged the kind of intellect you get with many working dogs, but that is part of the reason why Bulldogs are intelligent. When facing such a large and intimidating opponent, they had to learn how to survive the encounter.

Today, that translates into a dog that is ripe for entertainment. They may not look like they have much in the brains department, which is something they can use against you if you aren't careful. It gets them out of additional work and training. Some of them can be very stubborn as well.

The best way to get a Bulldog to behave and do what you want them to do is to train them. You will need to be very patient with your Bulldog, even during those stubborn fits, but in the end it is worth it. For example, you can definitely teach a Bulldog to play fetch, with the hardest part of the training being to get them to drop whatever they have fetched. They may try to get you to play tug of war instead, or they may just want to keep holding onto their toy. When they aren't doing what they are told, it isn't out of malice, it's just a personal preference that you have to train them to stop doing.

Photo Courtesy of Amy Savarino

Loving Loungers

Most Bulldogs are perfectly content to lounge with their people on the couch. There is no better way to pass the day than with a healthy breakfast followed by napping on the couch for hours with you by their side. It is a far cry from where the breed started out, but it is also understandable. This is definitely a breed that has earned its place as a couch lounger, and they want you to know that it is a good thing. Of course, you will need to be all right with the drooling and gas, but those are small prices to pay for such a unique and incredible companion.

When you are ready to do something a little more active, you will have to gear it to the Bulldog's abilities and the weather. Once the exercise is out of the way, you might as well follow it up with another meal and hours of lounging, right?

Given that Bulldogs can't exercise as much as other dogs in the same size range, you will need to be careful not to overfeed your Bulldog. This can prove to be challenging if you snack on the couch and your Bulldog sneaks food from your plate or bowl. You will need to monitor your Bulldog's weight over time to make sure it stays in a healthy range. Since they have poor heat regulation of their bodies, Bulldogs really cannot carry any extra weight.

They Go Where You Go

"They will make you laugh with their funny antics. When you talk to them they will tilt their head like they can understand what you are saying to them. They love and need their family. Don't be surprised if they follow you everywhere in the house, even into the bathroom where they may just sit there and stare at you."

Sheila Wright
Baysidebulldogs

This part is absolutely no joke. You may be accustomed to small dogs following you around the home, but there aren't many dogs among medium-sized dogs that will follow you quite like a Bulldog.

Sheila Wright of Bayside Bulldogs pointed out that it can be difficult to find privacy with a Bulldog: "They love and need their family. Don't be surprised if they follow you everywhere in the house, even into the bathroom where they may just sit there and stare at you."

This is also a good thing if you like to travel. Bulldogs are not particularly territorial – it is family that is important to them. If you want to go on a vacation or a year-long trip, your Bulldog is happy just being with you wherever you go. They will pretty much sleep during the entire trip, waking up to look around or for the occasional bathroom break. You won't find many other dogs that will be quite so content traveling as the Bulldog.

CHAPTER 4
Finding Your Bulldog

If you have reached this part of the book, you are probably starting to feel really excited about the possibility of getting your Bulldog. Whether you were interested initially because of a mascot, a friend who has one, or were just curious, if you have been thinking that a Bulldog sounds perfect for your lifestyle, it is time to learn about what you need to look for in your Bulldog.

You have several important decisions to make, starting with deciding if you want a puppy or a rescue. There are advantages and disadvantages to both. It is also important to do as much research as possible before adopting either because one is a lot of time dedicated to training, while the other is a lot of time dedicated to getting to know the dog's personality.

Photo Courtesy of Kirsty Hazell

Adopting From A Breeder

All purebred dogs come with established health problems that are fairly well documented. Breeders should be well aware of the risks, and great breeders will be upfront about the problems. They will also keep track of their dogs so that they can provide details to prospective puppy parents about the genetic history of each puppy. Proper breeding and tracking of the parents can help to breed puppies that are far less likely to suffer from the ailments that are common in Bulldogs.

Finding A Breeder

Finding the right breeder takes a considerable amount of time because there are many considerations when looking for a purebred puppy. Take some time to research breeders online and see how they have ranked. You want to find someone who is fully invested in the puppies and is willing to dedicate time to helping you be the best puppy parent possible. Their interest is in finding a good home for their puppies. The interest that a breeder takes in the puppy after it leaves home is indicative of how well cared for the parents are and how healthy the puppy will likely be.

The first thing you need to do when looking for the right breeder is to look for someone who clearly loves their dogs and is willing to put in the extra effort and attention to raise them right. They should begin some of the initial training too. If you find someone who posts regular pictures and information about the parents and the progress of the mother's pregnancy and vet visits, that is a very good sign. The best breeders will not only talk about their dogs and the plans for the parents in the future, they will stay in contact with you after you take the puppy home and answer questions as they arise. These are the kinds of breeders who are likely to have waiting lists and posts about their puppies and the information their new families provide. The active interest in knowing about what happens to the puppies later shows that they care a great deal about each individual dog.

You will need to plan for hours of research and prepare a list of questions for each of the breeders you talk to. It is likely that for each breeder you call, the conversation will last about an hour. That is for each breeder you contact. If a breeder does not have time to talk and isn't willing to talk with you later, you can cross them off of your list. After you have talked with each of your possible breeders, compare their answers.

The following are some questions to ask.

Photo Courtesy of Guillermo Arango

- Ask each breeder about the required health tests and certifications they have for their puppies. These points are detailed further in the next section, so make sure to check off the available tests and certifications for each breeder. If they don't have all of the tests and certifications, you may want to remove them from consideration. Good breeders not only cover all of these points, they offer a guarantee against the most harmful genetic issues.

- Make sure that the breeder always takes care of all of the initial health requirements in the first few weeks through the early months, particularly shots. Puppies require that certain procedures be started before they leave their mother to ensure they are healthy. Vaccinations and worming typically start around six weeks after the puppies are born, then need to be continued every three weeks. By the time your puppy is old enough to come home, the puppy should be well into the procedures, or even completely through the first phases of these important health care needs.

- Ask if the puppy is required to be spayed or neutered before reaching a certain age of maturity. It is possible that you may need to sign a contract that says you will have the procedure done, which you will need to plan for prior to getting your puppy. Typically, these procedures are done in the puppies' best interest.

- Find out if the breeder is part of a Bulldog organization or group. Many of these have minimum requirements that must be met for all of their members.

- Ask about the first phases of your puppy's life, such as how the breeder plans to care for the puppy during those first few months. They should be able to provide a lot of detail, and they should do this without sounding as though they are irritated that you want to know. They will also let you know how much training you can expect to be done prior to the puppy's arrival in your home so you can plan to take over as soon as the puppy arrives. It is possible that the breeder typically starts housetraining (in which case, you are very lucky if you can get on the wait list with them). You will also want to find out if they can provide information on how the puppies have been performing and how quickly they have picked up on the training. You want to be able to pick up from where the breeder left off once your Bulldog reaches your home.

- See what kind of advice the breeder gives about raising your Bulldog puppy. They should be more than happy to help guide you to doing what is best for your dog because they will want the puppies to live happy, healthy lives even after leaving the breeder's home. You want a caring breeder who is more interested in the health of the puppies than in the money they make. Yes, you could end up paying a considerable amount of money, but you should also get recommendations, advice, and additional care after the puppy arrives at your home. Breeders who show a lot of interest in the dog's well-being and are willing to answer questions during the dog's entire life span are likely to breed puppies that are healthy.

- How many breeds do they manage a year? How many sets of parents do the breeders have? Puppies can take a lot of time and attention, and the mother should have some down time between pregnancies. Learn about the breeder's standard operations to find out if they are taking care of the parents and treating them like valuable family members and not as strictly a way to make money.

Photo Courtesy of Chanda Barnes

Health Tests And Certifications

"I highly recommend you buy a pup from a breeder who does health testing. In the past few years there has been a big push by BCA 'Bulldog Club of America' to do health testing on breeders breeding stock. Reputable Breeders breed to better the breed and to breed to the Bulldog breed standard. At the very minimum test for heart, trachea, patella."

Kym Thew
Bullyful Bulldogs

This one is critical for the health of your puppy, and your breeder should be able to provide you details about the testing conducted prior to a puppy being placed. Benjamin De Jesus of Champion Bullies put it succinctly: "Genetic health issues can be minimized by getting a Bulldog puppy that comes from a breeder that breeds ethically and sticks to Bulldog standards. A good breeder will never breed a sire or dam that has health issues!" If a breeder does not give you this information, do not adopt from that breeder.

To start, you need to know what kinds of health problems Bulldogs tend to have. The following are the health tests required by the Bulldog Canine Health Information Center & Ambassador for Health Program:

- Patella Luxation (can be done through OFA)
- Cardiac Evaluation (can be done through OFA)
- Tracheal Hypoplasia (can be done through OFA)

They recommend the following tests:
- Hip and elbow dysplasia evaluations (OFA evaluation)
- Thyroid (can be done through OFA)
- Eye examination by someone who is a member of the ACVO Ophthalmologist (they should be registered with either the OFA or the CERF)
- Autoimmune Thyroiditis
- Congenital Deafness
- Hyperuricosuria
- Cystinuria

Breeders who are members of a Bulldog association, club, or organization are already showing that they are serious about ensuring that their

Photo Courtesy of
Kathleen Marks

dogs and puppies are healthy. Being a member of a Bulldog organization requires that a set of requirements are being met, so it shows that they are reliable and predictable in the way they treat the puppies.

For more information, you can visit OFA.org. Bulldogs that are not properly bred can suffer from many ailments, so you need to take the time to find a breeder who tests their breeding Bulldogs and the puppies.

Contracts And Guarantees

Contracts and guarantees are meant to protect the puppies as much as they are meant to protect you.

If a breed has a contract that must be signed, make sure you read through it completely and are willing to meet all of the requirements prior to signing it. The contracts tend to be fairly easy to understand and comply with, but you should be aware of all of the facts before you agree to anything. Beyond putting down the money for the puppy, signing the contract says that you are serious about how you plan to take care of the puppy to the best of your abilities by meeting the minimum requirements set forth by the breeder. Since they focus on your behavior toward taking care of your dog, it is a good sign that breeders want to verify that you are serious about taking care of your puppy. It is probable that the contract will include spaying or neutering the puppy once it matures. It may also say that the breeder will retain the registration papers of the puppy, although you can get a copy of it.

The guarantee states what health conditions the breeder guarantees for their puppies. This typically includes details of the dog's health and recommendations on the next steps of the puppy's care once it leaves the breeder's home. Guarantees may also provide schedules to ensure that the health care started by the breeder is continued by the new puppy parent. In the event that a major health concern is found, the puppy will need to be returned to the breeder. The contract will also explain what is not guaranteed. The guarantee tends to be very long (sometimes longer than the contract), and you should read it thoroughly before you sign the contract. Guarantees are fairly common with Bulldogs because of how old the breed is. The guarantees state what the breeder is guaranteeing with your new dog. This usually includes information on the dog's health and recommendations on what the pet owner's next steps should be. For example, it may recommend that you take your puppy to the vet within two days of arriving at your home to ensure that the dog is as healthy as it is believed to be. In the event that a major health concern is found, the puppy will need to be returned to the breeder. It will also explain what is not guaranteed.

In addition to the price of getting your dog, Bulldog contracts ensure certain behavior by the new human parent of a Bulldog puppy. Bulldog contracts usually come with a requirement to have the dog spayed or neutered once the dog reaches maturity (typically six months). The contract may also contain naming requirements, health details, and a stipulation for what will happen if you can no longer take care of the canine (the dog usually goes back to the breeder). They also include information on what will happen if you are negligent or abusive.

Puppy Genetics – The Parents

Good breeders always take the parents' history very seriously and track vet visits and other data points. This is particularly true if the breeder is part of an organization. You will want to review each of the parent's complete history to understand what traits your puppy is likely to inherit. Pay attention to their learning abilities, temperament, clinginess, and any personality trait you consider important.

This could take a while, but it is always well worth the time you spend studying and planning for the puppy. The more you know about the parents, the better prepared you will be for your puppy. The great breeders will have stories and details about the parents so that you can read about them at your leisure, as well as getting a good feel for the breeders.

Selecting Your Puppy

"You should be able to go to the breeder's house once the pups are old enough to see the pups as well as both parents (if possible). You want to see the environment in which you pup was raised. You have to be so very careful these days with all of the puppy mills and people that are breeding for all the wrong reasons."

Kym Thew
Bullyful Bulldogs

You want to have a visual of your puppy before you bring your new family member home. See if the breeder will provide videos and pictures so that you can check out your puppy after it is born and as it grows in the first few weeks after birth. You also want to get any data on your dog's vet visits and shots.

Selecting a Bulldog puppy is pretty much the same as picking any kind of puppy. A lot of it is entirely up to you and what you want in a dog. The

experience can be highly entertaining and enjoyable – and ultimately very difficult. As much
fun as it is, you do need to be
careful and serious so that you
are not swayed by traits that
you may find bothersome later.

As you look over the pup-
pies, notice how well each puppy plays with the others. This is

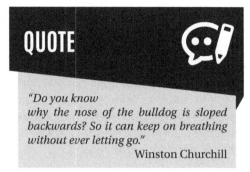

QUOTE

*"Do you know
why the nose of the bulldog is sloped
backwards? So it can keep on breathing
without ever letting go."*
                                    Winston Churchill

a great indicator of just how well your puppy will react to any pets you already have at home.

You also need to look at the puppies as a whole. If you notice that a ma-
jority of the puppies exhibit aggressive behavior or seem to tend toward
being mistrustful, you may not want to select a puppy from the litter. Simi-
larly, if the puppies appear to be terrified of you, such as keeping their tails
tucked or shrinking away, that is an indication of the kinds of issues you
may encounter with your puppy and training. What you want is a litter that
is full of friendly puppies, even if they do not start to greet you immediately. Sometimes they just want to play with their siblings or figure out what is
happening before acknowledging you.

Next, notice if there is at least one puppy that is very eager to meet you.
Many people take that as a sign that the puppy is the right one for their
family. However, that is not always the case. Keep in mind that the puppy
or puppies that greet you are more forward and demanding than the ones
that sit back and analyze the situation first.

The puppies that hang back may be afraid, or, more likely, they just
want to understand the situation before they get involved. They are not the
alpha types that their eager siblings are. These are your more patient and
tame puppies, ones that may be easier to train.

Pick the puppy that exhibits the personality traits you want in your dog.
If you want a forward, friendly, excitable dog, the first puppy to greet you
may be the one you seek. If you want a dog that will think things through
and let others get more attention, this is mellower dog that may be better
for your home.

Adopting An Older Dog

The one thing that is universal about puppies is that they are a lot of work. If you miss a day or two of training it may feel like you are back to square one. Older Bulldogs can offer you a way to get your Bulldog without having to dedicate several years to training. You can find older Bulldogs in shelters, rescues, and even from breeders. Breeders will take back puppies if a person does not treat the dog well or if a person can no longer take care of the Bulldog for some reason.

Benefits

Older dogs give you more immediate gratification. You don't have to go through those sleepless nights with the new puppy or the endless frustration that comes with early types of training. Older Bulldogs let you get right into enjoying your dog as you go out on adventures together. All intelligent dogs require a lot of time and attention as puppies. Bypassing that is a major part of the appeal of older dogs.

Older Bulldogs not only have the basic training already done, many of them already know tricks, so you can start exploring the world of what they know and what they still have to learn. This is an incredibly rewarding, funny, and enjoyable experience, just like getting to know a new friend. You can also start your own training. This part is nearly as much fun because the older Bulldogs have the attention span and ability to learn incredibly fast (if they are in the mood), and you will be able to recognize when they are ready to learn and when they are disinterested in the activity.

Better still, they can help you start improving yourself. If you want to get more exercise, an older Bulldog will help you get started immediately (instead of trapping you in the home trying to teach him the basics). You also have a wide range in possible activities, and your Bulldog will be more than happy to join you as you explore new places or get a new look at old ones.

Adult Bulldogs are ideal for individuals and families who do not have the time or patience to work with a puppy.

Rescues

The Bulldog clubs have their own rescue groups, in addition to their own breeders. Bulldogs that you get through the organizations and breeders have most of the necessary information that is required to sell puppies, meaning you will have the medical history and vaccination information on the dog (although if the human parent was negligent or abusive, the medical history and information may not have been tracked while the dog was with them).

It is very easy to contact the organization to see about adopting an adult Bulldog. They will require you to apply for the adoption simply because they want to ensure that the dog gets a great home – a place where the dog will be able to live out the rest of his or her days. They will also try to match you up with an adult dog that is ideal for the environment you offer and the life-style you live.

Warning About Socialization

Bulldogs that are not properly socialized at an early age can show signs of aggression as they age, and this may make them unsuitable for your home. For a breed with the kind of history that Bulldogs have, you have to be very cautious about rescuing a Bulldog without having any history on the dog. You do not know how it was socialized or what kind of experiences it has been through. This can make them challenging in the beginning, and you will need to dedicate as much time to monitoring your Bulldog as you would a puppy. They are going to be nervous, and that increases the chance that they will be aggressive. Depending on what they have been through, there are situations that you will definitely want to avoid with your Bulldog.

Introduction To Children And Other Pets

Introducing a rescue Bulldog to your home is a bit different than intro-ducing a puppy because you probably don't have a complete history of the dog. As personable as they are genetically, if a Bulldog is not properly social-ized, introducing a rescue to children and pets can very risky.

Rescues may not have much or any history on a Bulldog, in which case you will not know exactly what to expect when you bring your Bulldog home.

As Benjamin De Jesus of Champion Bullies said, "Adults may or may not get along with other dogs. It all depends on what environment the Bulldog was previously raised in, something you will never know if you get a dog from a rescue or shelter." If the people taking care of the dog prior to you adopting it cannot tell you about the dog's past or how the Bulldog has in-teracted with other dogs and animals in the shelter, you probably do not want to bring the Bulldog home if you have children and other dogs. It is very risky if a Bulldog has had negative experiences. These dogs are better suited to a single person or a couple without pets and who have the time to dedicate to learning about the dog and helping to socialize it as much as possible. It definitely takes as much patience and understanding as with a puppy, but you also have to be constantly aware of your surroundings. If you can't do this, look for a rescue Bulldog with a known history that is ac-customed to a life like the one you can provide.

CHAPTER 5
Preparing For Your Puppy

Preparing for your Bulldog puppy can create a whole atmosphere of excitement. Once you have found the right breeder and are waiting for your puppy, or as you are looking to rescue an adult Bulldog, you likely have a few days to more than a year to wait. Fortunately, that preparation is going to fill all of that time.

Getting your home ready for a puppy is going to take you just as much time as preparing for a baby – it's just that your furry baby is going to be mobile a lot sooner. You should plan to spend a good bit of time and money preparing before the new family member arrives. Though it isn't the most enjoyable aspect of what is to come, being thorough in your preparation is definitely worth the time and effort you put into it. Making sure your new Bulldog has a safe space with all of the essentials (especially the toys) will make the puppy's arrival a great time for everyone – especially your new canine companion.

Photo Courtesy of
Jan Toogood

46

Photo Courtesy of
Lisa Phan

Preparing Your Kids

Bulldog puppies are absolutely adorable, but they are not nearly as sturdy as adult Bulldogs. They are incredibly playful and do not know their limitations. Your kids will need to be careful when playing with the puppy, particularly younger children. Putting rules in place can begin as soon as you decide to adopt a Bulldog puppy or adult Bulldog. You will need to adopt a method of implementing the rules based on the age and understanding of your child or children. Preparing a toddler for the addition of a puppy is significantly different from preparing a teen. Still, the rules that you need in place apply to everyone, even you.

You will need to introduce the rules to your children as soon as you decide to bring a puppy into your home. Then you will need to periodically review the rules so that your kids know them inside and out before the puppy arrives.

Make sure to set aside some time on the day of the puppy's arrival for one final review. When your kids start playing with the puppy that first time, you will need to be present to reinforce those rules. Remember to be very firm so that the puppy is not hurt. You will need to be present for these interactions for the first few weeks, but the first time is particularly important as even teenagers can get carried away playing with an adorable little Bulldog puppy.

The following are the five golden rules that you want to make sure your children follow from the very first interaction.

1. Always be gentle. Bulldog puppies are absolutely adorable, but they are still puppies, which means they are fragile. At no time should anyone play rough with the puppy (or adult Bulldog since they will pretty much go along with whatever you want to do).

   This rule must be applied consistently every time your children play with the puppy. Be firm if you see your children getting too excited or rough. You don't want the puppy to get overly excited either because puppies may end up nipping or biting. It isn't their fault because they haven't learned better yet – it is the child's fault. Make sure your child understands the possible repercussions if they get too rough.

2. Chase is an outside game. It can be easy for children to forget as they start to play and everyone gets excited. That short game of getting away can quickly devolve into chase, so you will need to make sure your children understand not to start running. Once they get outside, chase is perfectly fine (though you will still need to monitor the playtime).

   Running inside the home is dangerous for two primary reasons. It gives your Bulldog puppy the impression that your home isn't safe inside because they are being chased, or worse, they get hurt. Or your puppy will learn that running inside is fine, which can be very dangerous as they get older. One of the last things you want is for your adult Bulldog to go barreling through your home knocking people off of their feet because it was fine for them to do that when they were puppies.

3. Always leave the puppy alone during mealtime. This is true whenever your puppy is eating (this can apply to when your kids are eating as well since you don't want your Bulldog to get accustomed to eating people food when your kids are eating). You don't want your Bulldog to think that anyone is trying to take the food away. Bulldogs aren't typically aggressive, so it isn't likely they will nip or bite because someone is near their food. However, they can feel insecure about eating if they feel like someone may take their food, which is obviously not fair to your Bulldog. And older Bulldogs could be a bit more protective of their food, which could lead to some conflicts. Save yourself, your family, and your Bulldog trouble by making sure everyone knows that eating time is your Bulldog's time alone.

4. The Bulldog should always remain firmly on the ground. This is something that will likely require a good bit of explaining to your children as Bulldogs look a lot like toys, especially Bulldog puppies. No one should be picking the puppy up off the ground. You may want to carry

your new family member around or play with the pup like a baby, but you and your family will need to resist that urge. Kids particularly have trouble understanding since they will see the Bulldog more like a toy than a living creature. The younger your children are, the more difficult it will be for them to understand the difference. It is so tempting to treat the Bulldog like a baby and to try to carry it like one, but this is incredibly uncomfortable and unhealthy for the canine. Older kids will quickly learn that a puppy nip or bite hurts a lot more than you would think. Those little teeth are in-

Photo Courtesy of Kaylee Fernandes

credibly sharp, and you do not want the puppy to be dropped. If your children learn never to pick up the puppy, things will go a lot better. Remember, this also applies to you, so don't make things difficult by doing something you constantly tell your children not to do.

5. All of your valuables should be well out of reach of your children, even your teens. Valuables are not something you want to end up in the puppy's mouth, but that is almost guaranteed to happen if you leave jewelry where someone can easily pick it up. Teenagers are just as likely to grab whatever is within easy reach to play with the puppy, so they are nearly as much of a threat to your valuables as tweens and kids who are older than toddlers. If your kids get curious, they are not likely to stop to consider if they should be doing something because they want to know what will happen if they use something to play with the puppy. The end result will be an incident that will certainly not make you happy, nor your children when you get upset with them. If you don't want your puppy or children to destroy something valuable, make sure it is never easily accessible.

Preparing Your Current Dogs

If you already have a canine or two of your own, they will need their own time to be prepared for the puppy's arrival. Of course, you can't go about it quite the same as with kids. There are no rules that you can tell your dogs, but there are definitely things you can do to prepare them. Once you have set the rules for the kids, you can start preparing your current furry companions. Your primary focus is to start adjusting your schedule so that you can let your dogs know that you still love them. You are going to need to make time for just them every day to accomplish this.

Here are the things you can do to help ease the transition to having a new Bulldog around the home.

- Think about your dog's personality to help you decide the best way to prepare for that first day, week, and month. Each dog is unique, so you will need to consider your dog's personality to determine how things will go when the new dog arrives. If your dog loves other dogs, this will probably hold true when the puppy shows up. If your dog has any territorial tendencies, you will need to be cautious about the introduction and first couple of months so that your current dog learns that the Bulldog is now a part of the pack. Excitable dogs will need special attention to keep them from getting overly excited when a new dog comes home. You don't want them to be so excited they accidentally hurt the new Bulldog.

- Consider other times when you have had other dogs in your home and how your dog reacted to these furry visitors. If your canine displayed territorial tendencies, you are going to need to be extra careful with how you introduce your new pup. If you haven't invited another dog to your home, you need to have a couple of play dates with other dogs at your home before your new Bulldog arrives. You have to know how your current furry babies will react to dogs in the house so you can properly prepare. Meeting a dog at home is very different from encountering one outside the home.

- Think about your dog's interactions with other dogs for as long as you have known the dog. Has your dog shown either protective or possessive behavior, either with you or others? Food is one of the reasons that most dogs will display some kind of aggression because they don't want anyone trying to eat what is theirs. Some dogs can be protective of people and toys too.

Puppies need their own designated areas for eating, sleeping, and re-siding when you are not spending time with the little guy. If you cannot give your puppy your full attention, your puppy should be in this area. This is im-portant if you have another dog or dogs because they will not be allowed in this area. Make sure that none of your dog's favorite toys, furniture, and other items are in this puppy's area. Make sure your children also under-stand to never put your dog's stuff in the puppy's area.

When it is time for your dog and puppy to meet, you will need to choose a spot that is not your home. You need to find neutral ground so that your dog does not feel territorial when the puppy arrives. Neutral ground gives your dog and puppy an opportunity to know each other prior to coming home.

When you introduce the pair (or more if you have multiple dogs al-ready), make sure you have at least one other adult with you. If possible, have your entire family present, but you need at least two adults for the meeting. If you have multiple dogs, you should have one adult per dog, and then one for the puppy. This will make it much easier to keep all of the dogs under control, because even if your dog's reaction is excitement, you don't want them to be too overwhelming for the puppy. The person in charge of the home must be present too. Part of that first meeting is about teaching the puppy the pack hierarchy.

Depending on how many dogs you have and their personalities, this meeting could take a while. The friendlier and more accepting your dog is, the easier it will be to incorporate the new puppy into your home. You will need to keep your puppy in the puppy area until all of the first round of shots is complete, and you should never leave your puppy alone with your dog or dogs until your puppy is older. It may take a couple of months for more protective and difficult dogs to be all right with the new addition.

The puppy adds a completely new dynamic to your home, and your dog may not be entirely happy with this energetic little puppy. That puppy's ar-rival completely changes your dog's life, and your dog is going to need some time to get accustomed to it. The older your dog, the less likely a puppy is going to be welcome. Given your older dog's limited abilities, the poor soul may get cranky with an overenthusiastic puppy with boundless energy. Old-er dogs may be less tolerant of puppies that don't follow the rules. You want your puppy to feel welcome and safe while making sure your dog knows that you still love him just as much as ever.

The same rules apply, no matter how many dogs you have. Think about the personalities of all of them as individuals, as well as how they interact together. Just like people, you may find that when they are together your

Photo Courtesy of
Eileen Ferrari

dogs act differently, which you will need to keep in mind when they are around the puppy. The introduction may need to be done with one dog at a time so that you do not overwhelm the puppy. Introducing each dog one at a time will help them calm down a bit before bringing all of the dogs together at the same time.

Your dog and the puppy will need to be kept apart in the early days, (even if they seem friendly) until your puppy is done with vaccinations. Puppies are more susceptible to illness during these days, so wait until the puppy is protected before the dogs spend time together.

Dangerous Foods

Humans and their close canine companions may have a lot in common, but digestion is not one of them. There are a number of foods that are safe for a human than can be dangerous or fatal to a dog. While it is fairly common knowledge that dogs shouldn't eat chocolate, it is less well known that they should not eat onions and grapes.

With a breed like the Bulldog, this can be problematic because they tend to want to eat everything. As Benjamin De Jesus of Champion Bullies said, "Bulldog puppies like to pick up everything, like vacuums." Considering how those sad eyes are going to look at you while you are eating, you have a very good reason to ignore your pup and keep the food to yourself. Since they are a medium-sized dog, small amounts likely aren't fatal, but you should still avoid letting your Bulldog have any of the foods on the Dog Do Not Eat List.

The following is a list of foods that you need to make sure your Bulldog can never get to as they are potentially fatal if consumed by a dog.

- Apple seeds
- Chocolate
- Coffee
- Cooked bones (they can kill a dog when the bones splinter in the dog's mouth or stomach)
- Corn on the cob (it is the cob that is deadly to dogs; corn off the cob is fine, but you need to make sure your Bulldog cannot reach any corn that is still on the cob)
- Grapes/raisins
- Macadamia nuts

HELPFUL TIP
Hold the Xylitol

It's no secret that dogs love peanut butter and, in moderation, peanut butter can be a healthy addition to your dog's diet. When choosing a peanut butter for your dog, try to avoid excess added salt or sugar, and do not purchase peanut butter made with xylitol. Xylitol is a popular artificial sweetener that is toxic for dogs but safe for humans. Xylitol can cause hypoglycemia in dogs, so be sure to contact your veterinarian immediately if you think your dog has consumed xylitol.

- Onions and chives
- Peaches, persimmons, and plums
- Tobacco (your Bulldog will not know that it is not a food and may eat it if left out)
- Xylitol (a sugar substitute in candies and baked goods)
- Yeast

In addition to these potentially deadly foods, there is a long list of things that your dog shouldn't eat for health reasons. The Canine Journal has a lengthy list of foods that should be avoided. It includes foods like alcohol and other things that people give dogs because they think it is amusing. Remember that dogs have a very different metabolism and the effect that these foods have on them is much stronger than the effect they have on people, even a dog as big as Bulldogs.

For the sake of your Bulldog's health, it is best just to keep all of these foods out of reach, even if the items are non-lethal.

Hazards To Fix

"Make sure you have a safe area prepared for your new puppy away from house plants, electrical cords, anything you wouldn't want him to get into. Many things that seem harmless are actually dangerous to a new puppy. Landscaping mulch is one of those very things, it seems quite harmless and yet there are chemicals in that mulch that could make your puppy very sick."

Melissa Riley
Stone Quarry Bulldogs

Just like you need to spend a lot of time preparing your home for an infant (and a lot more for a toddler), you are going to have a lot of things to fix prior to your Bulldog puppy's arrival. Bulldog puppies are small enough to get into places that you would not expect given how big the dog will be. It is going to take you a good bit of time, so make sure you set aside at least a full month to go through your entire home (more time is better if you have months to prepare).

This section details the areas of the home where you should really focus your attention to make sure you don't miss anything important that could be dangerous for your little darling.

Also, be aware that Bulldogs (puppies in general) will try to eat virtually anything, even if it isn't food. Nothing is safe – not even your furniture. Puppies will gnaw on wood and metal. Anything else within their reach is fair game. Keep this in mind as you go about puppy-proofing your home.

Kitchen And Eating Areas

Easily the most dangerous room in the house, the kitchen is a combination of poisonous foods, dangerous items, and poisons. It is the room where you should probably plan to spend most of your time when puppy-proofing your home. Everything you would do to protect a small child in this room is something you will need to do for a Bulldog. This could include making sure the cabinets are locked in case your Bulldog is clever enough to figure out how to open them. They are going to be following you around like a little shadow once they are allowed out of their puppy area, and they will be learning that things open. Some of them are clever enough to be able to get into cabinets, especially the cabinets where you do not want them to go.

You will need to make sure that all poisons are put in places where your Bulldog cannot reach them (whether in the kitchen, in other rooms of the house, the garage, or in outdoor areas). Bulldogs can get into nearly everything, and they will be exploring a lot when given the opportunity. Anything that may catch your attention or draw your interest is worth a try – that's what centuries have taught them. Being vigilant about making sure they can't hurt themselves is vital to keeping your Bulldog safe. At no time should you leave poisons in an unsecured place in your kitchen or other area.

Trash cans are equally dangerous because that's where all kinds of great smells exist to lure your Bulldog to misbehave. Having just gone over the list of foods that they shouldn't eat, having any of these foods in the trash is a serious risk to a Bulldog puppy. There are also things like poisons, plastics, and other items your puppy may think should be taste tested. Just because your Bulldog is small does not mean that it is impossible for him to knock over a trash can. Take all of the necessary precautions, such as getting a trash can you can lock or storing it under a cabinet that is locked. This will keep your puppy from getting into too much trouble or creating a mess for you to clean up.

All electrical cords need to be up and out of reach of little Bulldog puppies that could be curious as to what cords are and how they work. Bulldog puppies are notorious for chewing on cords – just as much as rodents. As Melissa Riley of Stone Quarry Bulldogs pointed out, "Make sure you have plenty of chew toys and a safe area prepared for your new puppy away from house plants, electrical cords, anything you wouldn't want him to get into."

Then there are things like blender cords and other wires that connect to heavier items that you don't want pulled onto your puppy. Cords aren't just electrical either – if you have long cords for your blinds, these need to be shortened or put where they will not fall to the floor where your Bulldog can reach them.

Bathroom And Laundry

The dangers in the bathroom are almost the same as those in the kitchen, just in a smaller space. There are so many poisons in bathrooms that keeping the doors closed could be the best way to go. Since that is really not an option for many families (particularly if you have children or teenagers who are likely to forget), you need to make sure to keep everything that could attract attention and danger locked up or out of reach.

Do keep the toilet seat closed, and don't use any automatic cleaners. Some Bulldogs have been clever enough to learn how to drink out of toilets, which means it is up to you to keep the toilets inaccessible to your curious pup. If the toilet seat is left open (as is bound to happen occasionally), make sure there aren't any poisons in it by avoiding having any automatic cleaners in the water.

Though it doesn't at first seem likely, the laundry room can actually be a dangerous room as well. The easiest way to deal with it is to keep the door shut if you can. Many families keep a number of miscellaneous items (including poisons) in the laundry room because it is a kind of catch-all place. You may only have bleach, laundry detergent, dryer sheets, and other clothing cleaners, but even those can be very dangerous to a Bulldog. This is particularly true of items like laundry pods. You also need to keep all dirty clothing off of the floor – if for no other reason than to keep your Bulldog puppy from dragging the most embarrassing garments all around your home. There is also a chance that your Bulldog may try to eat some of the clothing, which would not be great for your Bulldog. Nor is it a great time for you as you have to take an emergency trip to the vet's office or animal hospital.

Other Rooms

Most of the other rooms of the house should be relatively safe since people don't tend to keep chemicals outside of cabinets.

You will need to do a thorough inspection for cords that are low to the ground or within jumping distance of your Bulldog's reach. All of these will need to be secured well above where your Bulldog can go. Don't forget about spaces like the computer area and entertainment center where there is typically a lot of wiring. You will also need to check the window cords to make sure they are too high for your puppy to reach.

All cleaning products need to be stored some place that your puppy cannot go, too. If you keep objects like air fresheners on surfaces, make sure that these areas are not places where your Bulldog can go. Since most Bulldogs are allowed on couches and beds, you will need to clear off end tables and nightstands – and anything accessible from the furniture that contains chemicals.

If you have a fireplace, all cleaning supplies and tools will need to be stored in a place where the puppy cannot get into them. The area where the fire is also needs to be made inaccessible to curious puppies. This needs to be true all of the time so that your puppy does not play in the ashes or with the wiring in the fireplace.

If you have stairs in your home, they will need to be cordoned off so that your puppy cannot try to go up or down them. Tables (including end tables and coffee tables) need to be cleared of dangerous objects, such as scissors, sewing equipment, pens, and pencils. All valuables should be kept in safe locations away from furniture where your puppy will go.

If you have a cat, you are going to need to keep the litter box off of the floor. It needs to be somewhere that your cat can easily go but your Bulldog cannot. Since this could include teaching your cat to use the new area, it is something you should do well in advance of the puppy's arrival. You don't want your cat to be undergoing too many significant changes all at once. The puppy will be enough of a disruption – if your cat associates the litter box change with the puppy, you may find your cat protesting the change by refusing to use the litter box.

Garage

The best way to deal with the garage is to make sure your Bulldog cannot go into it. There are so many dangerous things in garages that keeping puppies out is the best policy. However, given their size, it is certain that the little Bulldog will manage to slip into the garage when you don't expect it. With all of the chemicals, sharp implements, and other dangerous tools that are stored there, the garage is one of the most hazardous places in any home. Never leave your Bulldog alone in the garage, even when it is an adult. It is likely that your puppy will be in the garage when you take car trips, which is why it is important to puppy-proof it.

All items related to your car and its maintenance have to be stowed high off the ground where your puppy cannot go, and a locked area is the safest way to store it. This includes all lubricants, oils, and cleaners, as well as wrenches and tools. You will need to do the same for all of your lawn maintenance items, bike tools, and anything used for heavy machinery or that includes chemicals.

Bulldog puppies will chew anything, including tires, cans, tools, and bags. The things in a garage look like fun toys or potential food, making them all fair game from a puppy's perspective. Everything that can be placed up high or locked in a cabinet should be.

You will need to do this with all of your hobbies too. Things like fishing tackle are incredibly dangerous and should be stored somewhere out of reach, too. You will need to make sure there is nothing hanging over the countertops where the puppy can try to pull it down.

The best way to tackle the problem is to enter the garage from a toddler's perspective. Anything that you would immediately move for a toddler should be moved for your puppy. Get down low and see the garage from your puppy's perspective. If you keep your cars in the garage, you can move them out to get a better view. Move anything that could be a potential danger.

Outdoors And Fencing

Your puppy should never be outside alone because there are too many hazards, even after you puppy-proof it. Keep in mind that you should never have your puppy outside of the designated puppy area without constant supervision. This is just as true in your yard as it is inside your home. Even if you have a fence, your puppy should not be left unattended when he is outside.

Puppy-proofing the yard won't be nearly as time consuming as puppy-proofing the inside. This doesn't mean that it isn't just as important though, especially if you plan to play with your puppy in your yard. Plan to spend between an hour or two outside inspecting and cleaning up in preparation for the arrival of your puppy.

The biggest dangers in the yard are the chemicals, mostly because people don't think about chemicals in the yard. Again, Melissa Riley of Stone Quarry Bulldogs warned why chemicals are so problematic: "Many things that seem harmless are actually dangerous to a new puppy. Landscaping mulch is one of those very things; it seems quite harmless and yet there are chemicals in that mulch that could make your puppy very sick. Gravel also is easily swallowed by a puppy and they can get sick and also choke..." As you prepare the outside, keep these things in mind and make changes as needed.

Begin by inspecting the fence to make sure there are no breaks, holes, or other potential problems. You will also need to look for areas that dip under the fence that would be easy for a dog to make bigger. Make sure to have all problems with the fence repaired and fill in holes under the fence. You want to make sure the cute little puppy can't escape, and given their size, it won't take much for them to slip through or under the fence.

Determine where in your backyard you want your puppy to go to the bathroom. You will want to make sure this area is cleared of all potential dangers because your puppy is going to be spending a good bit of time in the spot every day. All poisons and dangerous tools need to be stored elsewhere, such as in a shed or a secure place in the garage. If you have objects like a birdbath or other artificial structures in the puppy's bathroom area, move it somewhere else. Of course, it is easiest to select an area that is already open and close to the door for rainy, hot, or cold days. It will be easier to maintain an area that is already clear.

Choose a different area in the yard for your puppy to play. Having a place for play and a place for going to the bathroom is important because you want the Bulldog to focus on using the bathroom in one place, and not be distracted by trying to play with you. This also lets your Bulldog know that it is time to play when you go to the different spot, which will make your little puppy that much more excited. Give this area the same inspection that you gave the housetraining space.

Stroll around the rest of your yard to look for other chemicals and dangers. All of them should be moved somewhere that you can secure them. Even with dedicated places for using the bathroom and playing,

Photo Courtesy of Andrea Young

your Bulldog is probably going to go to other areas of the yard, particularly if you have children. Make sure there is nothing dangerous in the entire yard.

Make sure all of your current plants are safe for dogs. Puppies will just as happily chew on plants as toys, making it essential to ensure there is nothing that can harm them.

Secure all water sources, such as pools, ponds, and streams. If you have a fire pit or grill, make sure it is secure so that your puppy cannot access anything potentially dangerous.

Just like the garage, inspect your yard as if you were a toddler. Keep your eyes open for anything that could be interesting to a Bulldog, then determine what is too dangerous to remain.

Supplies And Tools To Purchase And Prepare

Planning for the arrival of your puppy includes buying all of the necessary supplies, like a crate, food, toys, and brushes. Start buying these things a month or two before your puppy arrives so that you can break up the cost over time. Bringing home a puppy can get very expensive; spare your budget by breaking the expenses up over a long period of time.

- Crate
- Bed
- Leash
- Doggy bags for walks
- Collar
- Tags
- Puppy food
- Water and food bowls (sharing a water bowl is usually okay, but your puppy needs his or her own food dish if you have multiple dogs)
- Toothbrush
- Brush
- Toys, especially chew toys

Feel free to add anything else you think of or want to have when your puppy arrives. Health care items like flea treatments can be purchased (they are expensive), even though you won't be able to use them for a while. Puppies should not be treated until they reach the specified age.

Planning The First Year's Budget

The budget for having a puppy is a lot more expensive than you would think – it's still less expensive to bring in a puppy than a new infant. You will need to have a budget, which is another reason to start purchasing supplies a few months in advance. When you buy the items you need, you will begin to see exactly how much you will spend a month. Of course there are some items that are one-time purchases, such as the crate, but many other items you will need to purchase regularly, like food.

You also need to have a budget for the one-time purchases too. This means doing some research ahead of time for those purchases. It is almost guaranteed that you are going to overspend, but you want to stick to the budget as much as possible.

Begin budgeting the day you decide to get your Bulldog puppy. The cost will include the adoption cost, which is typically higher for a purebred dog than for a rescue. If you want to rescue a Bulldog, you should figure out where you want to find your newest family member. Plan to spend a lot of time researching costs for bringing your puppy home, as well as the other costs.

The vet and other healthcare costs should be included in your budget. Regular vaccinations are required, and an annual checkup should be included in the budget. Vet prices vary a lot between different states, even between cities, making it difficult to average the cost. It is always worth the cost, but you want to know what it will be before your puppy arrives.

There are a lot of activities that you can do with your dog. Bulldogs are great pets because you will pretty much always want to enjoy your Bulldog without ever leaving home. A simple Google search yields pages of recommendations on ways to entertain and to be entertained by your new family member. The Bulldog community is worldwide, and people who have had Bulldogs tend to adore their dogs and are constantly thinking of new ways to enjoy the company of their canine companion.

Keep Things Out Of Reach

Bulldogs are going to be right there with you wherever you go, which means that they are going to be able to get to nearly everything within your reach. It is very important to keep a lot of things out of their reach, especially for the times when you are not home. They can knock things over, like plants and decorations. Bulldogs can have anxiety issues, and they may knock things over while trying to look out windows to see you.

The Puppy Area

When you set up an area for your puppy, it needs to be in a place that won't disrupt your current routines, especially for other pets. It would also be best to have an area where it will be easy to clean the floors. Your puppy is going to have a lot of accidents in those early days, and you don't want to have nice carpeting, rugs, or flooring ruined. It should also be close to where you sleep, unless you want to set up two puppy areas, one for the day and one for the night. Breeders also recommend that it be somewhere a bit quieter so that it isn't too overwhelming for the puppy in the early days.

Most breeders also recommend safety gates and fencing. You will need to test it to make sure that your puppy can't get out, and other animals and children cannot get into the area. Donna Moreno of Saint Brides Bulldogs recommends "baby gates and a good sturdy crate 36 inches in length." This way the puppy will have a comfortable crate after growing up.

There should not be any furniture in the puppy's area either. Given their penchant to chew anything and everything, you want to make sure that the only thing constantly in their reach is their puppy paraphernalia. A few safe toys, water, bedding, and maybe a blanket that is difficult to tear up should be the only things in the puppy area.

CHAPTER 6
The First Week

Photo Courtesy of
Sabrina Alcantara

The moment your Bulldog puppy comes through that door, everything changes. Years later, you will still remember just what happened, and it will be a story that you tell within the family. Your Bulldog is going to be the center of attention whenever he is in the room, and nearly everyone will love playing with or cuddling up to such a rough-and-tumble-looking couch potato. On the day your puppy arrives, you should know that you are committing to rearing your puppy – puppies are a lifetime commitment that is always worth the effort to raise them right.

The first week is going to be very difficult for your Bulldog puppy, and it is critical to the development of your puppy. During this time, your puppy will start to establish the dynamic in the home and you want your puppy to begin to feel safe in a new environment. These are the early days of seeing your Bulldog reach his full potential. With all of the puppy-proofing already done, it's time to start teaching your puppy how to play. This is going to be important as your Bulldog puppy is going to want to put his mouth on everything. You will also need to show the puppy where to go to the bathroom and prove that the home is a great place to live. This is when you really get to learn about the joys of having such a personable, loving, loyal dog in your home.

Preparation And Planning

Set aside time before your puppy arrives to go through to make sure everything is prepared. This final check of your home is to make sure everything is still secured and everything set up for the puppy. From the puppy area to food and toys, you should have everything set and ready for your puppy. Anything that you can do before the Bulldog's arrival will help you to better enjoy your time together when he gets there so that you don't have to try to do stuff on the fly – you are going to have to do that enough without leaving too many things to do for later. Start inspecting your home to make sure you didn't miss anything.

HELPFUL TIP

What About White Noise?

From babies to adults, people who have difficulty falling asleep often rely on white noise to tune out the world around them and help them get to sleep. If your new dog has trouble sleeping through the night, it's possible that white noise could help him too. There are a wide variety of white noises you can try, from nature sounds to electronically generated ones, so try a few and see what works to calm your puppy down.

You should do one more inspection from the ground level in every room of the house and the garage. This should be done a few hours before the puppy arrives to make sure that all of the risks have been removed (habits can be difficult to break, so make sure everything is in order). Make sure everything is properly puppy-proofed.

During the final week before the puppy arrives, create a list of everything that your puppy needs for the first day. The following should help you get started:

- Food
- Bed
- Crate
- Toys
- Water and food dishes
- Leash
- Collar
- Treats

Verify that you have everything on the list out and ready for use before your Bulldog walks through the door. You don't want to have to run out and buy them after the puppy is home, partly because you want those things to be readily available, and partly because you don't want to miss time with your newest family member and establishing a routine.

Photo Courtesy of Chanda Barnes

If you plan to have a fence to keep the puppy penned into a specific area of the home, have the gates set up and verify that it cannot be knocked over or circumvented. Your Bulldog puppy may try to make a break for it if there are any weaknesses or holes in the fencing around his designated area because your Bulldog is likely to try to get out to stay with you as much as possible.

Set up a schedule for the puppy's care. Know that the plans are going to change, but you need to have a starting point. This will ensure that people complete their assigned tasks and help to make your puppy feel safe – dogs prefer structure, so schedules are a great source of security for them. Tweak the schedule as it becomes clear that changes are needed, but try to keep it as close to the original schedule as possible. Having a schedule in place before the puppy arrives will make it a lot easier than if you try to establish something after the arrival. The Bulldog is going to have more than enough energy to keep you busy, making it difficult to make a plan after his arrival.

The schedule should include a bathroom break after every meal. There is a good chance your puppy will need to go then, and this will help establish where the right places are to use the bathroom.

Have a final meeting with all of the family members to make sure all of the rules are remembered and understood before the puppy is a distraction. Children will need special training in how to handle the puppy, and you are going to need to be very strict in making sure they aren't too rough with the pup. Verify that your children understand that they are not allowed to play with the puppy unless there is an adult supervising them. Determine who is going to be responsible for primary puppy care, including who will be the primary trainer. To help teach younger children about responsibility, a parent can pair with a child to manage the puppy's care. The child will be responsible for things like keeping the water bowl filled and feeding the puppy, and a parent can oversee the tasks.

Bulldog training happens from the moment your puppy is given into your care. The rules and hierarchy should start to be established from that first car ride home.

As tempting as it is to cuddle and try to make your Bulldog feel comfortable, you will need to put the Bulldog in a crate for the ride – you cannot start by making an exception. Your puppy is learning from the very beginning. Remember, this is a breed that has been living alongside humans for a very long time, and they know how to take cues from you. Anything that they can do to make you drop your guard and let them get away with stuff, they are going to use later. As difficult as it will be, you will need to be firm and consistent with your Bulldog puppy.

The Ride Home

Two adults should be present on the first trip. Ask the breeder if the puppy has been in a car before, and, if not, it is especially important to have someone who can give the puppy attention while the other person drives. The puppy will be in the crate, but someone can still provide comfort. It will definitely be scary because the puppy no longer has mom, siblings, or known people around, so having someone present to talk to the puppy will make it a little less of an ordeal for the little guy. Bulldogs may not tend to lean toward being a fearful dog, but that doesn't mean that they don't get scared.

Photo Courtesy of Nikki Crosnoe

This is the time to start teaching your puppy that car trips are enjoyable. This means making sure that the crate is secure instead of being loose to be moved around during the drive. You don't want to terrify the puppy by letting the crate slide around while the puppy is inside it, sitting helplessly. This kind of jostling will teach your Bulldog that cars are terrifying instead of making them feel safe.

Digestive Issues

The first day to first week is likely to be difficult for your puppy, and for Bulldogs that often manifests as digestive issues. Your puppy may have diarrhea or constipation, which will make them cry even more. This is normal for the first day, but consult the breeder if you have concerns. If it lasts for a couple of days, ask your vet during the first visit to make sure everything is all right.

First Night Frights

Photo Courtesy of Nora Kiss Burrows

That first night is going to be incredibly scary to your little Bulldog puppy. Away from mommy and any siblings, as well as the humans the puppy has come to know at the old home, it is understandable if the puppy is terrified. As understandable as this may be, there is only so much comfort you can give your new family member. Just like with a baby, the more you respond to cries and whimpering, the more you are teaching a puppy that negative behaviors will provide the desired results. You will need to be prepared for a balancing act to provide reassurance that things will be all right and keeping your puppy from learning that crying gets your attention.

You should have a sleeping area established for the puppy prior to the arrival. It should include a bed, and probably a crate or pen. The entire area should be blocked off so that no one can get into it (and the puppy cannot get out) during the night. It should also be close to where people sleep so that the puppy does not feel abandoned.

Things like sounds may attract your puppy's attention, and those unfamiliar sounds can be scary. If you can minimize the number of noises, this could help make the first night a little less terrifying. These noises may not be as noticeable to you, but dogs have a much better sense of hearing.

To make things a little more familiar, you could also request that something that smells like the mother be provided. The best way to get an item that smells familiar is for you to send a blanket along that the breeder can place with the mother for a few days before the puppy comes home. The blanket can then also travel with the puppy in the car on the way to your place.

Your puppy is certainly going to make noises over the course of the night, and you cannot think of them as an inconvenience (no matter how tired you are). The puppy is sad and scared, so you will just need to endure it. Do not move the puppy away from you, even if the whimpering keeps you awake. Being moved away from peo-

Photo Courtesy of Heather Clark

ple will only scare the puppy more, reinforcing the anxiety and fear of your home. Doing this on the first night will make the wrong impression, starting things off on the wrong footing. Over time, simply being close to you at night will be enough to reassure your puppy that everything will be all right.

Not getting much sleep should be something you expect during that first week or so (just like with an infant), but especially that first night. Make sure you don't have work or anything pressing to do the next day so that the lack of sleep isn't too disruptive. Losing sleep is part of the deal of bringing a puppy into your home. Fortunately, it doesn't take as long to get a puppy acclimated as it takes with a human infant, so your normal schedule can resume more quickly.

You will need to learn to ignore the whining, but that will get easier over time so that the puppy doesn't learn to do this every night. If you give in, over time the whimpering, whining, and crying will get louder. Spare yourself the trouble later by teaching the puppy that it won't work.

Do not let your puppy into your bed that first night – or any other night until they are fully housetrained. Once a Bulldog learns that the bed is accessible, you cannot train them not to hop up on it. If they are not housetrained, you are going to need a new mattress in the very near future.

Photo Courtesy of
Nick and Jenevieve D'Amico

The last thing that is going to cut into your sleep is the need for regular bathroom breaks. You can set up something in the puppy's space, or you can plan for trips outside every few hours (depending on how you plan to train your puppy). Whatever housetraining path you use, you are going to need to keep to a schedule even during the night to train your puppy where to use the bathroom. Puppies will need to go to the bathroom every two to three hours, and you will need to get up during the night to make sure they understand that they are to always go to the bathroom either outside or on the wee pad. If you let it go at night, you are going to have a difficult time training them that they cannot go in the house later.

First Vet Visit

This is going to be a difficult task because you may feel a bit like you are betraying your puppy (especially with the looks your puppy will give you during shots and the following visits to the vet). However, it is necessary to do this within the first day or two of your puppy's arrival. You need to establish a baseline for the puppy's health so that the vet can track progress and monitor the puppy to ensure everything is going well as the Bulldog develops and ages. It also creates a rapport between the Bulldog and the vet, which can help too. The initial assessment gives you more information about your puppy, as well as giving you a chance to ask the vet questions and get advice.

It is certain to be an emotional trip for your Bulldog, although it could be exciting in the beginning. Wanting to explore and greet everyone and everything is going to be something that your puppy is very likely to want to do. Both people and other pets are likely to attract your puppy's attention. This is a chance for you to work on socializing the puppy, though you will need to be careful. Always ask the person if it is all right for your puppy to meet any other pet, and wait for approval before letting your puppy move forward with meeting other animals. Pets at the vet's office are very likely to not be feeling great, which means they may not be very affable. You don't want a grumpy older dog or a sick animal to nip, hurt, or scare your puppy. Nor do you want your puppy to be exposed to anything potentially dangerous while still going through the shots. You want the other animal to be happy about the meeting (though not too excited) so that it is a positive experience for your puppy.

Having a positive first experience with other animals can make the visit to see the vet less of a scary experience, and something that your Bulldog can enjoy, at least a little. This can help your puppy feel more at ease during the visits.

The Start Of Training

Photo Courtesy of
Crystal McDermott

Your Bulldog's training begins the moment your puppy enters your car or your home, and it will continue for most of your Bulldog's life. The first few weeks will have some more intense training as you are teaching the basics, and this will serve as the foundation for all other training.

The focus during these first few weeks is to minimize undesirable behavior. Make sure to find out if the breeders started housetraining prior to the puppy leaving. Given how smart they are, your Bulldog may already be well on the way to being housetrained. If this is the case, you will need to follow the same routine that the breeder used. Consistency is important for your puppy to finish training.

The Leash

Leash training will probably be pretty easy since your Bulldog will be excited about anything that you want to do together. The training is actually just as much for you as for the puppy. You do not want to get used to dragging the puppy away from things that the Bulldog is sniffing. You will need to start finding ways to keep your puppy walking without being too forceful.

Given how excitable Bulldogs are, many breeders recommend that Bulldogs be trained to walk with harnesses. Your pup probably has not used one before, so there may be a learning period when they have to get accustomed using a harness instead of being able to move around freely like they do at home (their boundaries are marked by walls, doors, and gates, not something on their little bodies). Don't drag your puppy because that will make your puppy dislike walks. Instead, you can let the little puppy explore parts of your house while being supervised and wearing the leash. You will need to keep an eye on your puppy the entire time that you let them drag the leash around so that they don't get hurt or choked.

Teaching Respect

Respect is a part of training, even for a dog as affable as the Bulldog. Whatever behavior you teach now will be lessons that your Bulldog carries forward. You want to teach your puppy to respect you without fearing you. Consistency is the best way to do that. Do not make exceptions during the first week because you will be fighting that lesson essentially for the rest of your Bulldog's life.

Consistency

With smart dogs, you have to be consistent in your approach to training. They will pick up on the times when you don't enforce the rules, and they will start to try to make those exceptions the new rule.

Bulldogs can also be incredibly stubborn, so you don't want to let them know that they can get away with anything. You have to make sure they don't think that they are in charge. Letting them know in a firm and consistent manner right from their first day ensures they understand that you are setting the rules. Learning that the rules always applies will help them to learn faster.

Acclimation To The Home

Those first few days are going to be very scary for your puppy. Having a blanket or toy with the mother's scent can help, but you are going to want to keep an eye on the puppy. Puppies may have diarrhea because of discomfort and anxiety.

Bulldog puppies may also experience some problems with allergies to grass. Donna Moreno of Saint Brides Bulldogs mentioned that during the first few weeks puppies may have "belly rash caused by irritation of the grass. Best to rub the belly with Desitin."

CHAPTER 7
The First Month

Photo Courtesy of Abi Appels

After making it through that first week, things should start to go more smoothly and you should have at least a beginning of your routine. Odds are you are pretty tired from the training and less sleep – puppies are a significant change in your life.

But now you have an idea of how to work with the puppy and your schedule has started to emerge. The puppy's personality is becoming more obvious and you will have an idea of what will work to help motivate the little puppy. Make sure that you don't rely too heavily on food since your Bulldog won't be getting much exercise. Toys can be a great motivation because they love to chew on things, and getting a little extra time to play will help convince your puppy that following instructions is good. This will make the rest of the month a little easier than that first week.

Your puppy is going to be adorable, making it easy to feel that you don't have to be as firm or consistent. It isn't true though. Staying consistent is important for the puppy to understand that the rules always apply – and to learn what the rules are. Don't be fooled by that adorable face, because you must continue to be firm and consistent in your approach so that the training sticks. Bulldog can learn quickly, but none of them will do what you want them to do if you don't take a firm and consistent approach to training. Make training a daily exercise, if only for short periods of time to get your pup used to the idea of training. You should see some results of the training by the end of the month, although the results may not seem very big. Small steps must be taken to get your puppy to be the perfect companion.

FUN FACT
Meatball

Adam Sandler's English Bulldog, Meatball, was lovingly referred to as his "first son" by the American actor. He served as ring bearer at Sandler's wedding to Jackie Titone in 2003, and starred in the short film A Day with Meatball in 2002. Meatball passed away in 2004.

Photo Courtesy of
John Christian

Not Up To Full Strength

As much fun as you want to have with your puppy, that adorable little jester still has a limited supply of energy. You won't be able to go on long walks, let alone hikes with your puppy. The activities will need to be tailored to a puppy still learning about its abilities, mostly at home. There will be walks on leashes, but that is still largely a learning experience. If you have a yard, that can also be a great place to play. Still, most of your trips will be within a block or two of home.

Walks will need to be kept short and exercise to short periods of time, though you can have many exercise sessions over the course of the day. Typically, the exercise sessions will end with a nice puppy nap, meaning you won't be overly tired but will have time to do things you need to do without feeling like your puppy misses you. The puppy will still need to sleep in the designated puppy area because when that little pup wakes, you may not be in the room.

By the time the month wraps up, your puppy will have a lot more stamina. Over the course of the month, and subsequent months, you will need to adjust your schedule to accommodate longer walks and playing sessions. Longer exercise sessions mean fewer sessions, which can actually free up more time in your schedule. Just make sure to monitor your Bulldog's energy levels so that you aren't pushing for too long a walk or play session.

Setting The Rules And Sticking To Them

Bulldogs love to be with you, but they do prefer to do things that they enjoy, with minimal work. Since they are so cute and affable, you are much more likely to give in, thinking that you can train them later. This is something that your Bulldog is going to notice and use to get his way. Although you may feel that your puppy is too young for a firm approach, this is something you will need to fight against. Puppies need a firm approach, perhaps even more so as you are establishing a baseline. Exceptions to the rules should never be made in the early days if you want the training to stick.

By failing to keep your training consistent, you are setting yourself and your Bulldog up for a lot of contention since it will be difficult to convince your dog that you are serious. Inadvertently,

Photo Courtesy of Danielle Heilman

you have already taught your Bulldog that listening to you is optional. With the right look or action, the Bulldog can get you to lose focus.

Remember, they are mischievous, so training is important to keep them from hurting themselves or destroying your items.

A firm consistent approach with your Bulldog is best for all parties. Enjoying your puppy means making sure all of the rules are followed – those rules are there for a reason.

If you can manage to be firm and consistent over that first month, things could get a bit easier in the subsequent months. Keeping a level head and applying the rules without any exceptions paves the way for easier training going forward. There will be a trust and respect that is built up from being a great trainer who keeps all of the lines clear, making the rest of your time with your Bulldog so much more enjoyable.

Early Socialization

"Involving them around everyday household chores is a good way to warm them up to socialization. Like vacuuming, having the TV on loudly, and being around children playing."

Chanda Barnes
Barnesenglishbulldog

Bulldogs love to be surrounded by others, whether it is by other dogs or people, but this natural inclination has to be encouraged through early socialization. It will be far easier to socialize with your Bulldog than it is with many other breeds because they tend to be very mellow, as long as you plan for it. A socialized Bulldog will be a fantastic companion that can enjoy nearly every situation and make people in the family feel better at the end of a long day.

Despite their history, Bulldogs aren't not an aggressive breed; they love to sit around and enjoy doing nothing. However, there could be triggers that make them agitated. Failing to socialize a Bulldog could result in an aggressive Bulldog. Aggression in Bulldogs is often a result of fear or a desire to protect, which is why socialization is critical.

Some of them can also be territorial, which you can stop early by setting up play dates for your Bulldog with other dogs. If you have friends or other family members who have dogs, have them bring their dogs over to help train your Bulldog that other people and dogs are fun and exciting, and should be welcomed into the home if you are around when it happens.

Toward the end of the first month you can also start to socialize your Bulldog during the walks. This is best to do while having people with dogs visiting, or friends who want to join you. If you encounter a calm, friendly dog with people who are willing to let their dog say hello to your puppy, let the dogs meet. You will want to make sure that the dog is friendly, and that the people are all right with the encounter – do not just go up to the other dog without asking first.

Your Bulldog will also need to be socialized with people. This should be fairly easy because people are going to want to meet your puppy while you are out walking. Bulldog puppies are adorable and people are going to want to meet your little guy. Do be careful when you let people meet your Bulldog because you want it to be a positive experience for everyone. Anyone who wants to meet your puppy will need to follow the same rules. The puppy should not

Photo Courtesy of Rosa Mata

be picked up – all play should be with the Bulldog's feet firmly on the ground. Children should be kept as calm as possible so that they do not get carried away and be too rough with the puppy. The point of socialization is to help the puppy feel happy and excited about meeting new people and dogs, instead of teaching them that there are reasons to be afraid of leaving home.

It is too early to take your puppy to a dog park. The first month is all about learning more about the home and immediate area, and meeting people and dogs they are likely to encounter regularly. Your puppy also needs to finish all of the vaccinations before having a lot of exposure to other dogs, especially off of the leash. All socialization should be in an environment that you can control. Dog parks are barely contained chaos with the excitement and enthusiasm of dogs enjoying the freedom of being with other dogs.

You will need to be extra kind to older dogs and pets that you have in your home at this time. The puppy is definitely a strain on them for so many reasons. Have time in the schedule just for you and your older dog so that your dog doesn't feel that you don't care about him anymore. It will probably be best to keep older dogs and puppies apart for most of the first month.

Treats And Rewards Vs. Punishments

Training and treats are so closely thought of together that it can be difficult to consider anything else as an effective means of training your dog. Second to treats, people think of punishment as a way of dissuading dogs from undesirable behavior. Although these have been the typical methods used in training, there are serious problems with both, particularly with Bulldogs. Teaching a puppy proper behavior is a balancing act to make sure that you are firm, but not cruel, so you should provide rewards, but use something better than food.

As a mellow dog, positive reinforcement is the most effective way to train Bulldogs. Food is an obvious choice, but you have to be very careful not to overfeed your puppy. You don't want the little pup to get accustomed to eating too much, especially as they become adults and no longer have a rapid metabolism. Bulldogs are prone to overeating, and you don't want them to come to expect treats, because this could come to backfire later when you stop giving them treats for following commands. Starting with treats is best, but you should quickly begin using praise and extra petting as the primary form of positive reinforcement. You could even add some extra playtime after a training session if your puppy does very well. Since they love to chew on things, toys can be a great incentive.

Photo Courtesy of Lisa Ostrowski

Having your puppy's respect is also essential for successful training. If your Bulldog respects you, it will be much easier for them to accept positive attention instead of treats because they know you are in charge.

You may occasionally need to resort to punishment with your Bulldog, particularly if they nip or chew on furniture. However, you have to be careful not to train them to believe in things or actions that will make your life more difficult. Never use the crate as a place to punish your Bulldog – it should be a safe haven when your puppy wants to be alone or sleep. It is not a jail and you should not treat it as one. You can use time out instead to get your point (and disappointment) across to the puppy. It should be somewhere that the puppy cannot interact with you, no matter how much the dear barks, whines, or whimpers, but you should still be visible to your pup. You don't want to scare the puppy. The point is to let them know that you are still there but intentionally not interacting because of the puppy's actions. By denying them access to you without you disappearing, you are reminding them just why they need to behave.

Exercise – They Don't Need Much

"The rule of thumb is, you should never walk a bulldog farther than you're willing to pick him up and carry him home. But in all seriousness, bulldogs do need exercise every day, just not as much as most other breeds."

Melissa Riley
Stone Quarry Bulldogs

Bulldogs don't require much exercise, which makes them perfect if you don't like to go out to exercise. Walking in the early morning and evening is great to get them out of the house.

Photo Courtesy of Stella Quimby

Is also enough to spend time playing tug of war. Given their difficulty in breathing, indoor play is going to be safest for much of the year, particularly when it is really hot or really cold. Fetch is also great while giving them a way to practice many of their commands. This might be best to do in the yard when the weather is cool. If you play ball in the house, make sure that it is a safe area with carpeting so that the puppy doesn't get hurt.

Best Activities

Tug of war and fetch can be great games to make sure your puppy gets enough exercise and is entertained. Since they are intelligent and love to chew, you will want to switch out the games to make sure they don't get bored.

Bulldogs can also be incredibly entertained by laser pointers. They can bounce around and try to catch that laser, and you can stop when they start to pant heavily.

Other games like hide and seek and Simon says are great ways to help your puppy learn over time. With enough attention and games, you can have a very intelligent little Bulldog that gets all the necessary exercise and excitement from easy games.

Beware Of Heat, Be Careful Of The Cold

Bulldogs cannot handle the heat at all. They have enough trouble breathing, and overheating can result in the death of your Bulldog. Puppies and older Bulldogs also don't manage well in the cold.

Never leave your Bulldog outside. Not only will the climate be a potential problem, but you also don't want them to chew on anything in your yard.

CHAPTER 8
Housetraining

Photo Courtesy of Joanna Jaszczak

Housetraining is probably the thing that you are least looking forward to doing with your puppy. If you are lucky, the breeder may have already started the house-training. According to Sandra Fulton-Cooper of Bodanna Bulldogs, "A good breeder has taught your pup to stay clean. Potty training is consistency and repetition. Stick to a schedule." If you have found a good breeder, it is likely that you will be picking up where the breeder left off. You will want to continue the training in the same way as the breeder has been training the puppy.

Two rules should be followed during this time.

1. Your puppy is not to be left to roam the house free when no one is around to monitor the puppy. Your Bulldog won't be pleased with the idea of being in a soiled crate, so that is a deterrent from using the bathroom when you are not around.

2. Your puppy should have constant, easy access to the locations where you plan to housetrain. If you cannot provide this, you will need to have frequent trips outside as your puppy learns where he is supposed to do his business.

Once you have your training plan, be prepared to enforce all of the rules and restroom schedule. You have a few decisions to help you better prepare and plan for the task ahead of you.

Understanding Your Dog

Every Bulldog is different, so you are going to need to work with your puppy as an individual to figure out what works best. However, there are some things that are fairly universal for puppies. They almost always go soon after eating and drinking. As Melissa Riley of Stone Quarry Bulldogs recommends, "One of the first things your puppy will do when he wakes up is urinate. Puppies generally eliminate within 10 to 15 minutes of eating; they usually start to sniff around for a place to go before they actually do. Take your puppy to the same place to go every time, so they learn that is where you want them to go and always praise puppy afterwards."

It may take a while before your puppy understands just what you want in those early days if they have not had training prior to arriving in your home.

Photo Courtesy of Karin Williams

Consistency is key with all dogs, no matter their personality or breed. Food is a great motivator, but you need to stick with small treats, or a piece of kibble to keep the puppy from overeating. As your puppy shows signs of being motivated by seeing you happy (for example, they get excited when you do or react by wanting to play when you talk), start using praise as much as treats to reinforce the puppy using the bathroom in the right place.

You will need to tailor the schedule to your puppy's needs. To start, always plan to take the puppy outside to the bathroom after eating and sleeping. If you successfully get outside right after these two activities, you have a much better chance of getting the puppy to the right place to do business.

Key Words

All training should include key words, even housetraining. You and all family members should know what words to use during housetraining, and you should all be using it consistently. If you have paired an adult with a child, the adult should be the one using the keyword during training.

It would be best to watch a few videos providing some hints and tips on training and the words that are often used. You have to be careful not to select words that you use inside the home because you don't want to confuse your puppy. Selecting the right word is a lot trickier than you might think because you use some of the words in conversation more often than you might expect (particularly if you are potty training a child at the same time).

*Photo Courtesy of
Amanda Arteaga*

Inside Or Outside

Eventually you are going to need to train your Bulldog to use the outside only, but depending on the time of year and your individual Bulldog, it may be necessary to start inside. In the middle of a snowstorm is not the time to be teaching your puppy that going outside is required. It is also difficult to teach a Bulldog when it is extremely hot. Both of these conditions will make it far more difficult to train your Bull-

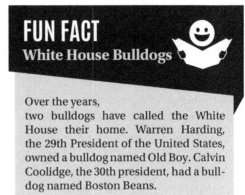

FUN FACT
White House Bulldogs

Over the years, two bulldogs have called the White House their home. Warren Harding, the 29th President of the United States, owned a bulldog named Old Boy. Calvin Coolidge, the 30th president, had a bulldog named Boston Beans.

dog to go outside. Be aware that if you have to start inside, you are going to need to purchase extra pads so that you don't run out. You will also need to expedite the timeline to train your puppy where the only acceptable places to go are in the home.

If you are able to start outdoor training, know that you are going to need to go out every two or three hours – including in the middle of the night. After a few weeks, you will be able to go outside less frequently, but in the beginning the best way to train is by going outside a lot so that your puppy learns to keep all business outside.

Puppies (and most dogs) tend to use the bathroom after waking up and after eating their meals. Even if it is out of the schedule, make sure you take your puppy out during these times because it is very likely the little guy will need to go. This will make it a bit easier to train him if you are telling your puppy to do something the Bulldog wants to do already.

If you have an area chosen for the restroom, teaching is easier. The Bulldog will begin to associate that area of the yard for one purpose. When you get there, the expectation will be easier to understand faster than if you let the puppy sniff around and go anywhere in the yard. It also makes it a lot easier to clean up the yard as you won't have to hunt for where the puppy went – it's all in one place.

Leashes can help in the early days too. If you gently lead the puppy to the area, it will become obvious over time that the Bulldog should go there to use the bathroom, then playtime might be in the cards.

They Are Intelligent – But You Still Need To Be Consistent

You have to be consistent in your approach to training a Bulldog so that they learn to listen to you. They are intelligent and stubborn, which means you really cannot make exceptions. You will need to plan for this based on when your puppy arrives so that you can keep them going to the same place to use the bathroom. If it is going to be too hot or cold, train them by having pee pads inside your home.

As difficult as it is, you need to take a firm, consistent approach, no matter how cute the puppy is. Fight the urge to consider something good enough or close enough. Your Bulldog needs to use the designated area and learn to hold it when inside. This won't happen if you make exceptions. Bulldogs watch you for cues, and if you send mixed signals, your Bulldog is going to opt for what is easiest.

Photo Courtesy of
Natasha Shaw

Positive Reinforcement – It's About Respect

"Give plenty of 'Good Boys' and treats when they go potty when and where they are supposed to."

Sheila Wright
Baysidebulldogs

Positive reinforcement works incredibly well for Bulldogs, even the puppies. Take a few pieces of kibble with you when you are teaching your puppy where to go. Learning that you are the one in charge will help teach the Bulldog to look to you for cues and instructions. They may try to push you a bit, to convince you that it's okay to let things slide because they want to enjoy time with you – not be forced to do something.

While you are being firm and consistent, when you puppy does the right thing, you have to lavish the little pup with praise. This is just as effective because Bulldogs love to see their people happy. They want to hear that they are good, and if you give them an extra treat or kibble, this will put them over the moon.

Knowing what you want will make it easier for your Bulldog to start to do things the way you want them done. By focusing on this aspect, you are establishing the respect needed for all future training.

Punishing your Bulldog is strongly discouraged. Punishment trains your Bulldog not to do something when you are around or to do it where you won't find it. The lesson you want to teach is not the one your Bulldog learns, so stick with positive reinforcement – they understand that very well. Training a Bulldog (or any dog) is not exactly like teaching a human, so you can't take the same approach.

Regular Schedule, Doggy Door, Or Newspaper

The last decision you need to make is how you plan to conduct the training. A good bit of the decision will be based on what you have already considered. Your Bulldog is likely to need to go to the bathroom after the following activities:

- After waking (both after naps and after night)
- After spending two or three hours in a crate or their puppy area

Photo Courtesy of
Bonnie Smith

- After eating
- While walking

Watch your Bulldog for cues and to determine what activities make the little pup have to go. Start tailoring your schedule around your puppy's unique needs.

Puppies have small bladders and little control in the early days. If you have to train him to go inside, there needs to be a single designated space, and you need to stock up on the appropriate pads for the puppy to have somewhere to go that isn't the floor. The pads are better than newspaper and can absorb more. You will need to plan to transition to the outside as quickly as possible before the Bulldog learns that inside is acceptable – this will be incredibly difficult to retrain later if you let them go inside for too long.

When out for walks is the perfect time to train your puppy to go. Remember, you can use a leash in the backyard to help get the idea of walks and potty across a little clearer.

It's All On You – Bulldogs Have The Brains, You Bring The Patience

Those brains can make training activities enjoyable, but it can be a problem with housetraining if your Bulldog is stubborn. Guillermo Arango of Bulldog Territory recommends, "Teach the puppy what it is allowed to do. Be consistent, patient, and correct it when it does something wrong."

You will need to carefully monitor your puppy. They will usually give you some indication that they are looking for a place to go. Also, taking them to use the bathroom before going to bed and immediately after waking will make it easier to reinforce the activity.

Remember that going outside for the bathroom should be the only activity that you do while you are training. Don't allow for distractions or play. Go directly to the spot and ensure the puppy goes to the bathroom. They have to know that going out to a certain area is business only.

CHAPTER 9
Socialization And Experience

"Socializing your bulldog is a must! I tell my puppy owners at a minimum enroll in a Puppy Kindergarten Class so that they can be around other puppies and learn some basic obedience like walk on a leash, sit, stay etc."

Kym Thew
Bullyful Bulldogs

Photo Courtesy of
Carlene Newton

Bulldog puppies tend to want to do whatever is easiest around adult dogs. They don't tend to need to be the alpha dog as long as they are with their pack. If your puppy is particularly stubborn, training classes can help, and are a great place for your puppy to have some socialization time. You want your companion to be comfortable everywhere the two of you go, and that is the ultimate goal of socialization.

Despite how easy it is to socialize a Bulldog, you still have to plan for it. Without planning and a controlled environment, socialization can go very wrong, very quickly. If you keep things simple and under control, your Bulldog will learn to relax and enjoy the company of other people and dogs.

Benefits Of Socialization

It is always important to socialize dogs, even a dog as easygoing as the Bulldog. The benefits of early socialization are that it can make things that much more enjoyable for everyone involved, no matter what the situation is. A socialized dog will approach the world from a much better place than a dog that is not socialized.

Photo Courtesy of Eleonora Fontana

It's Easy

Bulldogs are not confrontational or aggressive, and they tend to think the best of everyone and everything. They are one of the ultimate go-with-the-flow kind of dogs, which will make socialization incredibly easy as long as you plan it. You want to make sure that you know the dogs that your puppy meets in the early days. After getting accustomed to those dogs, it will be much easier to teach your Bulldog that other dogs can be a lot of fun.

It will be even easier to get them accustomed to people. Many people are drawn to say hello to this very unique breed. They aren't entirely common, and there is no mistaking a Bulldog for any other breed. As long as people know the rules about interacting with your puppy, it will be great socialization when you do go out for a walk.

Problems Arising From Lack Of Socialization

Socialization starts the moment your puppy arrives. Without socialization, no amount of training is going to help your Bulldog better interact with other animals and humans. All other rules still apply during socialization, so keep that in mind while you help your dog meet new friends.

Puppies need to be allowed to learn how to interact with others so that they aren't always terrified or upset with you when there are other people or dogs around them. It isn't healthy for your Bulldog to always be anxious or nervous around others, especially when you can easily avoid it. Make

Photo Courtesy of Ginger Martin

time to socialize your puppy to make his life enjoyable so he is as happy to meet new people and dogs as you and your family are.

Why Genetics Matter

Genetics are important in terms of not only the dog's health but their personality. Bulldogs don't tend to be aggressive or unpleasant, but there are always exceptions. Early socialization can help bring out the Bulldog heritage of loving new people, dogs, and experiences. You will want to learn whether or not their parents are skittish or standoffish so you will know what to expect and can watch for those traits and correct them.

Photo Courtesy of Jayden Perks

Predictable Pet When Properly Socialized

Bulldogs are great when properly socialized and trained. They are often in the top of their class when they take training classes, and they love the praise when they do well. As a mellow breed, Bulldogs want to be able to just relax and enjoy the company around them. To have a fantastic Bulldog, you just need to make sure they are socialized when they are young.

Common Problems

Bulldogs don't typically have problems as long as they are socialized from an early age. They love almost any living creature if they learn not to be afraid when they are young. However, they can be aggressive if they are not properly socialized. With their history, you want to make sure that your Bulldog is socialized so that your dog and those who meet your dog are as entertained by the encounter as you are with your regular interactions with your Bulldog.

Photo Courtesy of Kaila Valle

Properly Greeting New People

It can be a lot of fun, so it isn't something most people avoid. (Who doesn't love meeting and playing with a lovable little dog?) The difficult part is finding the time to do it often enough to reinforce the positive behaviors and teach the puppy that the world is a fun place to live in.

Greeting new people is usually a pretty easy task outside of the home, but it can be a bit tricky when you are at home. Training your Bulldog how to treat visitors may take a little longer because he will very excited and will want to be the center of attention. In the end, it is worth the effort as your Bulldog becomes an enjoyable companion for you and anyone who visits.

STORY
Handsome Dan

Handsome Dan, the Yale University mascot, has a long history as school mascot, dating back to the 1890s. Yale was the first American university to adopt a mascot and as of 2019, there have been 18 "Handsome Dans."

Behavior Around Other Dogs

Bulldogs are an incredibly agreeable dog. They do not need to be the alpha dog, but they can believe that things should always be fun and exciting. If you have an older dog, most Bulldogs will be able to peacefully work out which one is alpha and which one isn't without too many problems. Since Bulldogs hate to be alone, it is probably better to have another dog if you are absent from the home for several hours every day.

CHAPTER 10
Being A Puppy Parent

"Bulldogs are very smart and learn very fast. Some of them are a little stubborn, but you just have to be consistent and be patient."

Guillermo Arango
Bulldog Territory

Photo Courtesy of
Madison Beauregard

It is incredibly easy to spend a lot of time just playing with puppies. Watching the way they react to everything is both highly entertaining and helps you to see the world from a different perspective. There is also a lot of work required being a puppy parent.

Bulldogs are gregarious and love to play, particularly if there is chewing involved. Getting them to take things seriously can be a bit trying at times because they just want to play or lounge about. If you are not consistent and firm, they are going to get the idea that you can be convinced to just have fun instead of focusing on work and training.

A well-trained Bulldog is one of the best companions you could ever have. It may take a while to get there since they can be stubborn, but it is more than worth the effort in the end.

Staying Consistently Firm

You have to be firm and consistent – all the time – when training any puppy, and Bulldog puppies are no exception. It is easy to give into that desire to just play, but you can't, especially in the early days. Once you get in the habit of letting your puppy get away with something, it will be very difficult to train them to take you seriously later. They are puppies, and that means maintaining the same approach to training all of the time. No exceptions.

Bulldogs can be difficult to train, not because of their intellect, but because of a different tendency. As Benjamin De Jesus of Champion Bullies points out, "Training can be a little more difficult as Bulldogs are very stubborn." If you aren't consistent, they are going to think that they don't have to listen to you.

Your puppy doesn't mean any harm when trying to gnaw on you, but you have to teach that puppy biting is wrong. It won't be nearly so cute later if they bite someone while trying to play. If you can gain their respect, you are still going to have your work cut out for you. It will be a lot easier though as they will learn to listen to you when you use your training voice, or no-nonsense voice.

Photo Courtesy of
Alexis Melton

Photo Courtesy of Erin Brett

Possible Problems With Bulldogs And Managing Behavior

Bulldogs tend to have great personalities, but that doesn't mean they are perfect. There are a few personality traits that you will need to watch for in your puppy.

Bulldogs can become protective of their food, so you need to train them that people may need to take their food bowl. Since Bulldogs tend to overeat when given the chance, you

QUOTE

"I'm a firm believer bulldog owners are kindred spirits. Mostly because we can and will have very serious conversations about snorts ... crusty eyes, crusty noses, puke, and various forms of gas with other bulldog owners."

Brad Pitt

want to make sure they don't become protective of food. You may need to take the food bowl away and help the puppy learn to be accepting of the bowl's removal.

Fun training sessions are a great way to get your puppy to learn. They are intelligent, which means they can get bored. By making the training sessions enjoyable, your Bulldog will have all the necessary motivation to keep learning.

Managing Gnawing And Chewing

All puppies will gnaw on anything they can get their little mouths around, but Bulldogs are notorious for chewing when left alone, are bored, or when they are puppies. Initially, they chew because of teething and chewing helps soothe the pain. They will gnaw on people or other animals as they learn how to play. It should be fairly easy to teach a Bulldog not to chew on people, but you are going to find it much more difficult to get them to stop chewing items.

While your puppy is teething you can give the little pup ice cubes. This not only gives them something to gnaw on, the cold will also help soothe the pain. Keep everything you don't want chewed out of their reach, including furniture.

For the first few months, keep the puppy in their designated area and keep everything they shouldn't chew out of that area. Toys and other items

Photo Courtesy of Marty Hanson

can be left in the area for your puppy to chew on when you are busy.

When outside the area, you will need to monitor the puppy's behavior. If the puppy starts to chew on something you don't want them mouthing, give them something that is acceptable to chew. Don't take your eyes off your puppy. As soon as you do, your little Bulldog is very likely to chew on anything in reach. If you can't keep a constant eye on the puppy, put the little guy back in the puppy space until you can.

Photo Courtesy of Jo Walker

Playtime!

Playing with a Bulldog is about as easy as waking up in the morning. All you have to do is move around and talk to prepare your dog for having a good time. Pull out a toy to get your pup really excited.

Spend a bit of time looking through everything that people have taught their Bulldogs. Those little couch potatoes are more than happy to learn to lounge, play fetch, and pretty much anything else you want to play. Their strength is in entertaining and spending time with you. Use that to find things that you really enjoy and that help you better bond with your Bulldog.

CHAPTER 11
Living With Other Dogs

FUN FACT
Semper Fi

Bulldogs have been adopted as the mascot for a number of sports teams, but did you know that a bulldog is also the unofficial mascot of the U.S. Marine Corps? The tenacity and courage of the bulldog were the inspiration behind a recruitment poster depicting a bulldog wearing a U.S. helmet chasing a dachshund in a German helmet after WWI. While there are a number of unofficial bulldog mascots in the Marine Corps, the most famous is Chesty. As of 2018, there have been 15 Chesty mascots.

More than nearly anything else, Bulldogs love being with their pack. They tend to be great proponents of just lounging about, but if you are up for some games, they will absolutely love that too. Short walks on a cool morning or evening are also incredibly welcome. And if you have other dogs, your Bulldog will love having them around too. They pretty much love everyone who lives with them, and they enjoy the company of strangers nearly as much. This is because they are just a very mellow breed.

Being left alone is something that they love a lot less. Bulldogs are not fans of being left alone, and to let you know they don't like it, they may decide to chew (or even eat) your furniture or anything else in their mouth's range. Since they don't love being alone, it is usually best to have at least one other dog around to keep them company. This will reduce their anxiety too.

Bulldogs may like to be lazy or playful (instead of being trained); they are much happier being with you and doing what you want to do over being alone. They don't have to be alpha, but they may have opinions on what you should be doing. And they definitely know how things should be going for them. They can be quite stubborn if what they want and what you want are not the same thing. If you aren't available, other dogs are a perfectly acceptable substitute and probably more willing to do what your Bulldog wants to do. Bulldogs do require socialization, and any other dog in your home will need some time to get accustomed to having a puppy or new dog in the house.

Introducing Your New Puppy

Your dog (or dogs) should meet your puppy in a neutral location. This will stop your dog from feeling territorial, though there may be some jealousy with a puppy being close to you. The jealousy will likely be minimized since the focus is going to be on the dog meeting the puppy. This means that your dog is going to be more interested in the puppy than probably almost anything else. The important thing is that the meeting is at a place that won't make your dog feel like the puppy is trespassing. No matter what

Photo Courtesy of Chanda Barnes

Photo Courtesy of
Haley Garland

breed of dog you have, the first meeting should always be introduced in a neutral place. Guillermo Arango of Bulldog Territory recommends that you "socialize the puppy with other pets, introducing it one to one. Never take a puppy the first time in a place where there are many dogs."

As your new family member and the rest of the canine pack start to get acquainted and feel comfortable with each other, you can head home. As they enter the home, they will have a bit more familiarity with each other, making your current dogs feel more comfortable with the new addition to the family. This sense of familiarity does not mean that they will be bonded, so there may be some tension, especially early on. This is why it is important to keep them separated when you aren't home. The puppy should be in the designated area, and it will be easier for your puppy to relax and start to get familiar with the new environment there. Since you set the special area up prior to your puppy's arrival, it will be much easier to start getting your puppy acclimated to his area.

Make sure that none of your other dog's stuff ends up in the puppy's area. This can be seen by your dog as a threat to his or her place in the pack and will generate unnecessary tension between your dog and the new puppy. The puppy will probably chew on anything and everything in the puppy's area, including things that belong to your other dog. At this stage, possessions don't mean anything to your little Bulldog. Your dog, on the other hand, will see this as a challenge, likely resulting in very negative behavior. This will be true when your puppy is out of the puppy area too. Make sure that all of your dog's stuff is out of the puppy's reach at all times. Before taking the puppy out of the designated area, make sure to do a bit of cleanup and store the dog's toys in a safe place.

Mealtime is another potential problem, so your puppy should be eating in a different location, at least in the beginning. Food tends to be the source of most dog fights and unnecessary tension. As your puppy gets older, you can start to feed your Bulldog with your other dogs, but keep them separated.

Your current dog probably isn't going to be happy about sharing you with the puppy either. Be prepared to make sure your dog knows you still care about him or her after the puppy arrives because your dog is going to be pretty uncertain with the new addition. Schedule one-on-one time with your dog, including longer walks, extra training, or general play. This will let your dog know that the puppy is not a replacement. Sheila Wright of Bayside Bulldogs recommends helping your current dog transition: "Introduce slowly and give the other pet a lot of attention so he or she doesn't feel threatened by the new puppy." You should start keeping a schedule with your dog so that you don't change the amount of time you spend together after the puppy arrives. It also means you will need to be just a firm and consistent with your puppy as you are with your dog. If you are more lenient with your puppy than with your dog, this will create tension between your dog and the puppy.

There are a number of benefits to having a dog in the home who already knows the rules. The biggest benefit is that your dog will also start scolding your puppy for misbehavior. Since your dog isn't likely to be swayed by how cute the puppy is, your dog will have a much more objective approach to training. Of course, your dog cannot be the primary trainer, but it is nice to have someone helping reinforce the rules and showing the puppy how things are done. Having a dog to set an example helps the puppy better understand where he or she is in the pack while learning what behaviors are unacceptable. As long as your dog is gentle with the new member of the family, it is all right to let your well-behaved dog scold and reprimand your puppy – just make sure there isn't too much aggression or roughness to the behavior correction. Having your own canine babysitter also helps establish a better relationship between the canines.

Should your dog opt out of this role, that isn't a problem either. There is no need to force a role on your current dogs because their behavior will be enough to show the puppy how to behave. It is best to let your dog decide what kind of relationship to have with the puppy.

Working Dog Mentality

Bulldogs love to have people and other dogs around. They are not great at being alone, and can be destructive when left alone. Having another dog in the home will help your Bulldog feel less anxious when there are no people around the home. They can become just as attached to other dogs as to people because they are not a picky breed. Their main focus is on having fun and relaxing – no matter who is present. As a breed with a history of working, they are accustomed to having peo-

*Photo Courtesy of
Patrick Mahon*

ple and other animals around. Being alone simply isn't something they enjoy at all.

The best way to keep your Bulldog happy is to make sure there is never any alone time. As your Bulldog ages, it is very likely that some alone time will be appreciated, but generally only on your Bulldog's terms. They will want to be able to escape for a bit, but still want people and dogs around for when they are ready to play or relax. As long as they can see you, they are going to be perfectly happy.

Biting, Fighting, And Puppy Anger Management

One of the reasons people do not want to start with a puppy is because of how challenging puppies can be. Bulldogs are typically even-tempered and adorable, but when it comes to chewing, they are horrible offenders. This means that they are going to chew on anything and everything that is within their reach. Since they have brains, that is going to include things they can knock over or off of stuff if you put items down in a way that the Bulldog can see it hanging over the edge. Fortunately, they are not tall, so if you put things up high and out of sight, your Bulldog isn't going to try to get it (most of the time).

Even a laidback puppy can instigate a fight when riled up, and that energy can really get on a dog's nerves (particularly older dogs). There will be times when even your Bulldog is not happy, and this may result in tantrums and lashing out at your dog. It isn't common, but that doesn't mean it won't happen.

An untrained Bulldog can be dangerous as they have to learn not to bite and chew on everything. They can also easily choke on things that are small if you do not teach them to drop stuff (trying to pry something out of a Bulldog's mouth is a Herculean challenge). To avoid this, you really have to start training your puppy early. Aggression isn't often a problem, but training can make sure that aggression isn't something your puppy adopts because there is no training to teach the puppy not to behave in that way. If you see your Bulldog starting to be aggressive (not just playing), immediately step in and let the puppy know that is not acceptable.

Photo Courtesy of Laurie Flash

Raising Multiple Puppies At Once

Only the brave puppy parents adopt more than one puppy at a time, and this is true even with dogs like the Bulldog. It is at least twice as much work and you will have to split your attention between two or more puppies at the same time. If you want to raise more than one Bulldog puppy at once, you are in for a real challenge. They are going to want to please you and spend time with you, but they are also likely to feel something similar for each other. They have the same energy level and desire to learn, which means that their misbehaviors can feed off each other. It will take a lot more energy and work to make sure they behave the way you want them to act.

Be prepared to lose your personal life, particularly your social life, if you have more than one puppy at a time. Taking care of those little puppies is going to be like having two full-time jobs. It is necessary to put a lot of work into training your puppies so that your home isn't destroyed twice as fast.

First, you must spend time with them both, together and separately. This does mean spending twice as much time with the puppies, making sure they get along well, learn at an even pace, and still get to have designated time with you. Each puppy will have its own strengths and weaknesses, and you need to learn what those are for each one, as well as learning how well the puppies work together. If they both behave during alone time with you, but tend to misbehave or fail to listen when they are together, you will need to adjust your approach to make sure they both understand the rules. This is a real challenge, especially if they whine when you are playing with one of them and not the other (which is very likely with Bulldogs).

You can always have someone else play or train with one puppy while you do the same with the other, then switch puppies. This builds bonds while letting the puppies know that they both have to listen to you and your training partner. Both puppies will also be happily occupied, so they won't be whimpering or feeling lonely while you are playing with the other puppy.

There may be some fighting between the puppies, and this is likely to start when they are between three and six months of age. They don't tend to be as aggressive as other dogs, but it is still almost certain that there will be minor fights. This is fine as long as they are not too aggressive. Likely it won't be because Bulldogs are less concerned with where they are in the hierarchy than in being with their people. As long as they understand the rules and abide by them, fighting should not be a significant problem with your puppies.

During training, you will need to minimize distractions, both for your puppy and yourself. This is why serious training should be done one-on-one more often than together. Puppies are always watching and learning, especially when you have a dog that is as enamored with you as the Bulldog tends to be. If you do not properly train them, it will be your fault when they become difficult adults who won't listen to you. Be consistent and focused during training to avoid the worst behavior problems.

CHAPTER 12
Training Your Bulldog Puppy

"Cute behaviors as a puppy may not be so cute as a 60 lb. adult, so make sure to decide if certain behaviors will always be acceptable or not and stick to it from day one. The rules apply the day you bring them home. There is no grace period or adjustment time. Set the rules immediately. Dogs understand better with consistency."

Sandra Fulton-Cooper
Bodanna Bulldogs

FUN FACT
Best In Show Winners

Bulldogs have been awarded the Best In Show title by the Westminster Kennel Club twice since the title was first awarded in 1907. The first bulldog to be awarded this title was Ch. Strathtay Prince Albert, owned by Alex H. Stewart, in 1913. The second bulldog awarded this title in 1955 was named Ch. Kippax Fearnought and was owned by John A. Saylor, MD.

Bulldogs can be a mixed bag when it comes to training. They are definitely smart enough to do well, but they have to want to because they can be incredibly stubborn. However, with a firm and consistent approach, your Bulldog will learn to respect and listen to you, which will make training a lot easier.

Working with a dog that should definitely be able to learn quickly but doesn't want to can be very tiring. By making sure to follow through with a few actions, you will find that your Bulldog will pick up on the training much quicker because there will be motivation to do what you want. Keep in mind that training your puppy is a long-term commitment. Even if your Bulldog isn't rebellious, the puppy probably just wants to have fun. Your puppy won't want to anger you, but gentle begging and puppy eyes can be very effective, and Bulldogs will learn that, particularly if you give in during a training session. That mug is absolutely adorable, and it can play off of that to try to get you to give in to his demands.

A Gentle, Consistent Approach

There are many times in life where you will feel something is close enough. This is never a good idea with intelligent dogs. They study their people and figure out ways to get what they want with as little work as possible. Wanting to please you will still drive a Bulldog, but if you are willing to give an inch, they will take it and see how much further you can be pushed. Exceptions and leniency are seen by your puppy as having some control over the situation, and that is not something you want them to learn when they are young. It just makes it that much harder to make them take you seriously later.

Photo Courtesy of Stephanie Barrett

Keeping a consistent and firm approach during training will make life for easier for you and your puppy. Even if you are tired at the end of a long day at work, you have to enforce the rules. No matter how cute or friendly your puppy is being, you must make sure that all of the rules you have been teaching him remain firmly in place. If you don't feel up to it, have a family member do the training. If you don't have anyone to help you, you can change up the training a bit to make it more enjoyable. It is fine to change things up if you are having a rough time, as long as you remain consistent. Interacting with your Bulldog can make for a much more enjoyable experience, and can even cheer you up. Consistency and firmness do not mean that you have to do the same thing all of the time. You just need to make sure that your puppy understands that you are in charge and there is no negotiating on that. This will keep your puppy on the right track to being a great companion instead of a little dictator.

Photo Courtesy of
Christopher Liley

Gain Their Respect Early

Being firm and consistent in your approach to training will start gaining you respect from your little canine early in your relationship. This is something you will need to keep building over time. Without respect, your Bulldog is going to think you don't mean what you say, and will start to try to get its own way. As long as you are firm and consistent, respect should be a natural part of the bond. That does mean that you cannot multi-task while you are training your puppy, or even just playing with your puppy. The Bulldog wants your full attention and will find a way to get it, even if it means breaking the rules to get your attention.

Positive reinforcement is the best way to gain respect, particularly if you use positive interaction. Playing with and training your puppy every day helps build a healthy, positive relationship that will teach your puppy where he or she fits into the pack. Your puppy learns that it is part of the family, but that you are the one in charge.

Operant Conditioning Basics

Operant conditioning is the scientific term for actions and consequences. What you have to do is provide your Bulldog puppy with the right consequences for each behavior.

The best way to use operant conditioning is through positive reinforcement, particularly since the Bulldog is so attached to people. This type of training is more effective with working dogs and dogs that have a long history with people because they want to please their people. They want to work with you and fulfill their tasks. Knowing that they are doing something right does a lot more to encourage their behavior than knowing when they do something wrong. With so much energy, they will be able to keep trying until they get it right.

Photo Courtesy of Ashley Richey

There are two types of reinforcements for operant conditioning:

- Primary reinforcements

- Secondary reinforcements

You will use both during your Bulldog training.

Primary Reinforcements

A primary reinforcement gives your dog something that it needs to survive, like food or social interaction. Both of these can be effective for Bulldogs – they love spending time with you and may be happy to have treats. That is exactly what makes treats so effective during training.

Initially, you will rely on primary reinforcements since you do not have to teach your Bulldog to enjoy them. However, you have to keep a balance. Mealtime and playtime should never be denied to your puppy, no matter how poorly the puppy performs. These things are essential to living, and you will have to give them the essentials – that is not negotiable. It is things like treats and extra playtime that you use to reinforce good behavior.

Err on providing too much attention and affection over too many treats. Because of their low exercise needs, Bulldogs need a well-balanced diet to be healthy. If you rely on treats instead of attention, you are setting yourself and your pup up for serious problems later.

Secondary Reinforcements

You used repetition to get good at your hobbies, sports, and other physical activities – this is secondary reinforcement. Without a doubt, Pavlov's experiment with dogs is the most recognizable example of secondary reinforcement. Using the bell, Pavlov taught the test dogs that when the bell rang it meant it was time to eat. The dogs began to associate the ringing of a bell to mealtime. They were conditioned to associate something with a primary reinforcement. You can see this in your home when you use a can opener. If you have any cats or dogs, they probably come running as soon as the can opener starts going.

Secondary reinforcements work because your Bulldog will associate the trigger with something that is required. This makes your puppy more likely to do as you tell it to do. Dogs that are taught to sit using only a treat will automatically react by sitting down when you have a treat in your hand. They won't even wait for you to tell them to sit. They know that sitting means more food, so they automatically do it once you make that association. Of course, this is not the proper training because they need to learn to sit when you say sit, and not when you have a treat. That is the real challenge.

Fortunately, it is relatively easy to train Bulldog puppies with the right trigger because they are both intelligent and eager to please. While they may enjoy food, you can show them that the trigger is the word, not the food. They will learn it much faster than many other dog breeds.

You can also use toys and attention as a way of getting your Bulldog to do the right thing. If you have a regular schedule and you are willing to change it a little to give your puppy a little extra attention for doing something right, that will be just as effective as a treat because they love attention. You can take the pup on an extra walk, spend a little more time playing with a favorite toy, or take some time to cuddle with the puppy.

Sometimes punishment is required too, but you need to be very careful about how you do it. Trying to punish a Bulldog can be tricky, but denying your Bulldog attention can work very well. Simply put your puppy in a penned off area where the Bulldog can see you but cannot interact with you. The little guy will whine and whimper to let you know that he or she wants out. Don't give in because this is the punishment. Just ignore your puppy to teach the lesson about proper behavior.

Punishments must happen right after the event. If your Bulldog chews something up and you don't find out for several hours, it is too late to punish the puppy. The same is true for rewards. To reinforce behavior, the reward or punishment must be almost immediate. When you praise or punish your puppy, make sure you keep eye contact. You can also take the puppy by the scruff of the neck to ensure that you keep eye contact. You won't need to do that when you are praising your pooch because he or she will automatically keep eye contact. Bulldogs can be absolutely driven by hearing your praise.

Why Food Is A Bad Reinforcement Tool

Bulldogs are not an energetic dog and they are not going to be getting too much exercise. They are also like bottomless pits – they will eat any food they can reach. Getting them accustomed to treats for training can result in your Bulldog becoming obese, which is incredibly unhealthy for any dog, but definitely for a dog that does not exercise much.

Kym Thew of Bullyful Bulldogs has a recommendation that could help: "If you have a Bulldog that is very food motivated (treats or even pieces of their dry kibble) you will have an easier time training them." Since Bulldogs don't tend to be particularly picky about their food, giving them a piece of kibble as a reward can help you keep from overfeeding your Bulldog, while keeping the Bulldog motivated to listen.

You will want to avoid high-calorie treats, and if you can get your Bulldog to respond well to praise, this will be best in the long run. It will be easier to do this when the puppy is still young because it can establish the right positive reinforcement while your puppy's metabolism is still high.

Small Steps To Success

Photo Courtesy of Giianna Lagorio

The first few weeks, or maybe even the first couple of months, are a time with a very steep learning curve. Your puppy is not going to understand what you are doing in the beginning as you try to convince your little Bulldog to use the bathroom outside. The best way to train the puppy is to realize that you need to start slow – don't begin with expectations that your puppy will be housetrained in a week (that won't happen). Your puppy must learn the daily routine (which you will be doing at the same time). Once the schedule and environment are less exciting, your Bulldog will have an easier time focusing during training sessions.

Training should begin from day 1. Even through your puppy is just getting to know the environment, you need to start putting some of the rules in place. As your puppy gets familiar with you and the environment, you can teach the Bulldog about its area and that the crate is for sleeping. Learning to go into the crate on command has some obvious benefits, particularly if you leave home every day. This is when you start using treats to train the puppy to go into the crate and do other basic activities.

Starting from day 1 does not mean trying to do everything – you must start small. Give treats for little things that your puppy might do anyway, like explore the crate. Once your Bulldog starts to understand the reward system, training will start to get easier.

Why Trainers Aren't Always Necessary, But You May Want One

Bulldogs do learn well, but it can be tricky. If you have the time and patience, it is always best to be your dog's trainer. They have to learn to listen to you.

However, given how stubborn Bulldogs can be, having them learn in a class structure will help them to see other dogs doing what they're told. Bulldogs tend to be at the top of their obedience class because the trainers can help you learn how to properly praise your Bulldog to keep motivation up.

Most of the time, Bulldogs just want to lounge around and have fun with you. If training can be enjoyable, that can be enough to convince them to start listening. A firm and consistent approach goes a long way to helping. If you have not trained a dog before though, taking a class can help you learn the right way to train your Bulldog. Losing your temper is not going to help anyone, especially your Bulldog. Trainers can show you the tricks that can help you gain respect from your Bulldog so that training is easier in the future.

If you have trained dogs before, you probably don't need a trainer. You do need to take a firm and consistent approach, with a focus on treats and knowing how to patiently work through your Bulldog's stubbornness (should it arise). Ultimately, your Bulldog wants to enjoy time with you, which is much easier if everyone knows the rules and abides by them.

CHAPTER 13
Basic Commands

Bulldogs aren't known for doing tricks, but once you get a Bulldog puppy in your home, you will see that they are definitely entertainers. If you can get your Bulldog puppy to start listening to you early on, you will find that your puppy will start to pick up all of the basic commands fairly quickly.

You definitely want to get your Bulldog to learn Leave It as early as possible considering how much and what Bulldogs will eat. Trying to get something out of a Bulldog's mouth is practically impossible, so you want to have the command to keep your Bulldog from picking anything up that could be potentially dangerous. This is the most difficult command on the list, but it is definitely possible to get your Bulldog to understand this command faster than many other breeds.

Photo Courtesy of
Trevor Kemerling and Tori Hiott

Why Their Personality Makes Them Ideal Companions

Bulldogs are happy just to be around you, wherever that happens to be. They will pretty much just sit by your side and follow you around the home making sure that you are always doing all right. They are like an incredibly noisy shadow that is always by your side. When you turn to look at them, those large eyes are just staring back at you, waiting for you to say something to them. They love interacting with you and any attention you give them will make them unbelievably happy. This is why they tend to do things that make you laugh. They love to see you happy, and they can't help but be incredibly entertaining.

Photo Courtesy of Erica Franklin

One of the things that breeders always bring up is just how much fun they have with their Bulldogs, which often comes as a surprise to people who don't know Bulldogs. Shelia Wright of Bayside Bulldog said, "They make you laugh with their funny antics. When you talk to them they tilt their head like they understand what you are saying to them."

Picking The Right Reward

One of the most interesting aspects of having a Bulldog is determining the right reward. You want to keep the treats to a minimum, which can be tricky. Treats may be a good starting point, but you will need to quickly switch to something that is a secondary reinforcer. Praise, additional playtime, and extra petting are all fantastic rewards for Bulldog pets since they care about how you feel and your reaction to them. Plopping down to watch a movie and letting the puppy sit with you will be a great reward after an intense training session. Not only did your puppy learn, but you both now get to relax and enjoy just chilling together.

If you begin to gain the respect of your Bulldog, that can be used to help train your dog. At the end of each session, give your puppy extra attention or a nice walk to demonstrate how pleased you are with the progress that has been made.

Successful Training

"Be consistent; teach one command at a time. Once they have mastered it move onto the next."

Donna Moreno
Saint Brides Bulldog

Training is about learning the commands. If your Bulldog learns to respond only to the rewards (such as the dog that sits as soon as you have a treat in your hand), the training was not successful.

Gaining the respect of your dog is generally the key in being a successful trainer, but with a Bulldog it also means dedicated attention – you have all of the puppy's attention during a training session. As you and your Bulldog work together, your dog will come to respect you (so long as you remain consistent and firm). Do not expect respect in the early days of training because your puppy does not have the understanding or relationship required to be able to understand. Fortunately, their intelligence will start to show early on, making it easy to see when they are starting to respond to you instead of just the reward. This is the time when you can start switching to rewards that are fun instead of those that center around treats and food.

Even in the beginning, you need to make handling and petting a part of the reward. Although your dog does not quite understand it for what it is, your Bulldog will begin to understand that treats and petting are both types of rewards. This will make it easier to switch from treats to a more attention-based reward system. Associating handling and petting as being enjoyable will also encourage your puppy to look at playtime as a great reward. No matter how much they love to eat, being entertained and playing with you will be a welcome reward since it means the puppy is not alone or bored.

FUN FACT
Otto the Skateboarder

Otto the bulldog set the Guinness World Record for longest human tunnel traveled through by a skateboarding dog. In 2015, Otto skateboarded through the legs of 30 people in Lima, Peru. Since setting this record, Otto has used his fame to get involved in charities and promote animal adoption. You can follow him on Instagram @OttoSkater.

120

Basic Commands

For the Bulldog, there are five basic commands that you must teach them, and ones that you will probably want to start training your puppy to understand. These commands are the basis for a happy and enjoyable relationship as your Bulldog learns how to behave. By the time your puppy learns the five commands, the purpose of training will be clear to your Bulldog. That will make it much easier to train them on the more complex concepts.

Photo Courtesy of
Victoria Gordon and Tyler Chmielewski

You should train the puppy in the order of the list as well. Sit is a basic command, and something all dogs, as well as your Bulldog, already do. Teaching leave it and how to bark less are both difficult and fight the instincts and desires of your Bulldog pooch. They are going to take longer to learn than the other commands, so you want to have the necessary tools already in place to increase your odds of success.

Here are some basic guidelines to follow during training.

- Everyone in the home should be a part of the Bulldog training because the Bulldog needs to learn to listen to everyone in the household, and not just one or two people.

- To get started, select an area where you and your puppy have no distractions, including noise. Leave your phone and other devices out of range so that you keep your attention on the puppy.

- Stay happy and excited about the training. Your puppy will pick up on your enthusiasm, and will focus better because of it.

- Start to teach sit when your puppy is around eight weeks old.

- Be consistent and firm as you teach.

- Bring a special treat to the first few training sessions, such as chicken or cheese.

Once you are prepared, you can get started working and bonding with your cute little Bulldog.

Sit

Once you settle into your quiet training location with the special treat, begin the training. It is relatively easy to train your dog to obey this command. Wait until your puppy starts to sit down, and say sit as he or she sits. If your puppy finishes sitting down, start to give praise and a small treat for it. Naturally, this will make your puppy very excited and wiggly, so it may take a bit of time before he or she will want to sit again. When the time comes and the puppy starts to sit again, repeat the process.

It is going to take more than a couple of sessions for the puppy to fully connect your words with the actions. In fact, it could take a little over a week for your puppy to get it. Bulldogs are intelligent, but at this age there is still so much to learn that the puppy will have a hard time focusing. Commands are something completely new to your little companion. However, once your puppy understands your intention and masters sit, the other commands will likely be a little bit easier to teach.

Once your puppy has demonstrated a mastery over sit, it is time to start teaching down.

Photo Courtesy of Ronnae Gold

Down

Repeat the same process to teach this command as you did for sit. Wait until the puppy starts to lie down, then say the word. If the Bulldog finishes the action, offer your chosen reward.

It will probably take a little less time to teach this command after you start training it.

Wait until your puppy has mastered down before moving on to stay.

Stay

This command is going to be more difficult since it isn't something that your puppy does naturally. Be prepared for it to take a bit longer to train on this command. It is also important that your dog has mastered and will consistently sit and lie down on command before you start to teach stay.

Choose which of these two commands you want to use to get started, and then you will need to be consistent. Once your dog understands stay for either sit or down, you can train with the second command. Just make sure the first position is mastered before trying the second.

Tell your puppy to either sit or lie down. As you do this, place your hand in front of the puppy's face. Wait until the puppy stops trying to lick your hand before you begin again.

When the puppy settles down, take a step away from the Bulldog. If your puppy is not moving, say stay and gives the puppy the treat and some praise for staying.

Giving the reward to your puppy indicates that the command is over, but you also need to indicate that the command is complete. The puppy has to learn to stay until you say it is okay to leave the spot. Once you give the okay to move, do not give treats. Come should not be used as the okay word as it is a command used for something else.

Repeat these steps, taking more steps further from the puppy after a successful command.

Once your puppy understands stay when you move away, start training to stay even if you are not moving. Extend the amount of time required for the puppy to stay in one spot so that he or she understands that stay ends with the okay command.

When you feel that your puppy has stay mastered, start to train the puppy to come.

Come

This is fourth in the series of commands since you cannot teach this one until the puppy has learned the previous commands. The other two commands do not require the puppy to know other commands to get started (it is just easier to train if the puppy already has an understanding of what commands are and how the puppy is expected to react to them).

Before you start, decide if you want to use come or come here for the command. You will need to be consistent in the words you use, so make sure you plan it so that you will intentionally use the right command every time.

Leash The Puppy.

Tell the puppy to stay. Move away from the puppy.

Say the command you will use for come and give a gentle tug on the leash toward you. As long as you did not use the term to indicate that the stay command was done, your puppy will begin to understand the purpose of your new command. If you used the term to indicate the end of stay, it will confuse your puppy because the Bulldog will associate the command with being able to move freely.

Repeat these steps, building a larger distance between you and the puppy. Once the puppy seems to get it, remove the leash and start at a close distance. If your puppy does not seem to understand the command, give some visual clues about what you want. For example, you can pat your leg or snap your fingers. As soon as your puppy comes running over to you, offer a reward.

Leave It

This is going to be one of the most difficult commands you will teach your puppy because it goes against both your puppy's instincts and interests. Your puppy wants to keep whatever he or she has in its mouth, so you are going to have to offer something better. It is essential to teach it early though, as your Bulldog is going to be very destructive in the early days. You want to get the trigger in place to convince the puppy to drop things.

You may need to start teaching this command outside of the training area as it has a different starting point.

Start when you have time to dedicate yourself to the lesson. You have to wait until the puppy has something in his or her mouth to drop. Toys are usually best. Offer the puppy a special treat. As the Bulldog drops the toy, say leave it, and hand over the treat.

This is going to be one of those rare times when you must use a treat because your puppy needs something better to convince him or her to drop the toy. For now, your puppy needs that incentive, something more tempting than what he or she already has before your puppy can learn the command.

This will be one of the two commands that will take the longest to teach (quiet being the other). Be prepared to be patient with your pup. Once your puppy gets it, start to teach leave it with food. This is incredibly important to do because it could save your pooch's life. They are likely to lunge at things that look like food when you are out for a

Photo Courtesy of Haley Garland

walk, and being so low to the ground, they are probably going to see a lot of food-like things long before you do. This command gets them to drop whatever they are munching on before ingesting it.

Where To Go From Here

These are all the commands that you are likely to need with your Bulldog. However, if you want your Bulldog to do tricks, you can pretty much go anywhere from here. These commands are the foundation of training, and the Bulldog is capable of learning so much more. Just make sure that the tricks that you teach your Bulldog are not too stressful for your puppy. As your puppy ages, you can start teaching tricks that highlight your puppy's agility. Fetch and other interactive tricks will be ideal because your Bulldog will want to do them.

CHAPTER 14
Nutrition

"Bulldogs suffer from flatulence. They fart... a lot. This is due to them eating too fast and taking in too much air as they eat. There are several food bowls in the market that will help with this eating issue."

Benjamin De Jesus
www.championbullies.com

Photo Courtesy of Cynthia Sanchez

Given how much Bulldogs love to eat, it is incredibly important to make sure that the food they eat is nutritious. It is just as important for your Bulldog to have nutritious meals as it is for you to eat healthy meals. Of course, you want to take good care of your Bulldog, and that can collide hard with that face begging you for some of that food on your plate. It will be difficult to say no, but you really, really need to learn to. Getting their diet just right is already a difficult balancing act. Fight that urge to fall into the habit of offering food that is decidedly unhealthy for your canine. From letting them have scraps from your plate to providing too many treats, many pets end up getting far too many calories for their activity levels. As your dog ages, this could become a serious issue for the canine's health. For Bulldogs, you even have to be careful about the kind of dog food you purchase. Ensuring your Bulldog gets the right nutritional balance is critical for a long, happy life.

Why A Healthy Diet Is Important

Since they tend to be pretty sedentary, overfeeding Bulldogs is incredibly easy. Their caloric needs for the day are fairly low. Many of the tricks and activities that they do can expend a good bit of energy, but that does not mean that they need a lot of food. If you have a very busy schedule, it will be entirely too easy to have substantial lapses in activity levels while you are home. Your Bulldog is still going to expect the same amount of food, regardless of activity level. This means they are likely to start putting on weight, which will be detrimental to their health.

Photo Courtesy of Madison Beauregard

You need to not only be careful of how much you feed your Bulldog during mealtime, but how many treats you offer over the course of the day. All food needs to be considered when you think about both nutritional and caloric intake. Because of their shorter, sturdier bodies, you need to be aware of roughly how many calories your dog eats a day. If you notice that your dog is putting on weight, you will be able to adjust how much food the Bulldog eats a day, or change the food to something with more nutritional value.

Breeders also recommend that you avoid food made of grains. Grains can make them gain weight faster. If you have the time, it is best to make your dog's meals – or at the least provide real food mixed with their dog food.

You should be aware if your puppy or dog has any specific dietary needs. The breeder or rescuer should be able to tell you if your Bulldog has any issues. Chanda Barnes of Barnes English Bulldogs points out that "some have grain allergies or require a special diet." Puppies will likely have tummy troubles in the early days, so that is not a sign that there is necessarily a problem. However, if your puppy continues to have problems, you should consult your vet. You can also find out what food the breeder gave the puppy and make sure to continue to feed your puppy the food it is accustomed to eating. This can help keep the tummy troubles to a minimum.

Commercial Food

Always make sure that you are buying the best dog food that you can. Take the time to research each of your options, particularly the nutritional value of the food. Be sure to account for your dog's energy level and age. Your puppy may not need puppy food as long as other breeds (or even other Bulldogs), and dog food for seniors may not be the best option for your senior Bulldog. To provide more nutrition, you can mix some food into the processed food. This can help supplement any nutrients, as well as being a healthy addition to an otherwise entirely processed meal. The addition of a little bit of home-cooked food with each meal will make your Bulldog excited to eat. Guillermo Arango of Bulldog Territory makes an easy recommendation if you are busy but want to add a little something special to your Bulldog's meal: "English Bulldogs are very easy to feed...Some of them are a little pikey with the food and we used to put a little peanut butter in the dry food and that works very well."

Preparing Your Food Naturally At Home

If you want to provide the healthiest meals possible, you should plan to spend an extra five to ten minutes in the kitchen per meal you prepare for your Bulldog. If you regularly make your own food (from scratch, not with a microwave or boxed meal), it really doesn't take that much more time to provide an equally healthy meal for your little companion.

Keeping in mind the foods that your Bulldog absolutely should not eat, you can mix some of the food you make for yourself in your Bulldog's meal. Just make sure to add a bit more of what your Bulldog needs to the puppy food bowl. Although you and your Bulldog have distinctly different dietary needs, you can tailor your foods to include nutrients that your dog needs. It won't really take that much longer to tailor a meal for you and a slightly different version for your dog. Read through Chapter 5 to make sure that you never give your Bulldog foods that could be harmful or deadly.

Do not feed your Bulldog from your plate. Split the food, placing your dog's meal into a bowl so that your canine understands that your food is just for you. The best home-cooked meals should be planned in advance so that your Bulldog is getting the right nutritional balance.

Typically, 50% of your dog's food should be animal protein (fish, poultry, and organ meats). About 25% should be full of complex carbohydrates. The remaining 25% should be from fruits and vegetables, particularly foods like pumpkin, apples, bananas, and green beans. These provide additional flavor that your Bulldog will likely love while making the little pup feel full faster so that overeating is reduced.

Puppy Food Vs. People Food

It is true that puppies need more calories than adult dogs. If you are bringing a Bulldog puppy into your home and know that you aren't going to have the time to cook, you should get food designed for puppies. This will ensure that your puppy gets the necessary calories for growth. Do not feed the puppy people food under the belief that you can switch to dog food later – because that is going to be virtually impossible. Once your Bulldog becomes an adult, it is nearly impossible to convince your canine that those unappetizing pellets are food, particularly when your dog knows what the food on your plate tastes like. Do not set a precedence that will create significant problems for yourself later. If you feed your Bulldog puppy food, you are going to have to keep making food for your dog once the puppy stage is a memory.

It is best to make your puppy's food if you can. There really isn't going to be that much of a difference in the amount of food between the puppy and adults stages. Their little bodies have special needs, and the first few months are critical. If you can make your puppy's meals (and know that you can keep it up when your Bulldog is an adult), this will be a lot healthier for your dog.

If you find that you have to start buying commercial food, you will need to start slowly mixing it into your adult dog's meal. Do not be surprised if you find the pellets are uneaten for a while. It will be a difficult process convincing your dog that this is food, but if you mix it with other things (and know that you are always going to need to mix at least a little real food in with the commercial food), your dog will be more likely to start eating it since it will smell like real food.

Dieting, Exercise, And Obesity

Your Bulldog is not going to diet the way you may choose to diet. This means you have to keep a regular eating schedule for your dog – their day is going to be based largely on the times of the day that are designated to eating. If treats and snacks are something you establish as normal early on, your dog is going to believe that is also a part of the routine and will expect it. Obviously, this can be a terrible habit to establish with your Bulldog, especially if it is food that you are sharing because you are snacking and feel guilty. You will need to make sure to be active after snacking so that your Bulldog doesn't get too many calories. An extra round of play or another walk can go a long way to helping keep your Bulldog at a healthy weight.

Photo Courtesy of
Alexis Melton

There needs to be a healthy balance of diet and exercise to keep your Bulldog from becoming overweight, certainly to avoid your dog becoming obese. Exercise is an absolute must. While you are helping your Bulldog develop healthy eating and exercise habits, you are probably helping yourself. Being more aware of your dog's diet and exercise levels will probably make you more aware of your own. Obesity is something that you will need to actively avoid with your largely sedentary pooch. Get used to exercising and playing as a reward system.

Warning About Overfeeding And The Right Caloric Requirement

You have to be careful of your Bulldog's weight, so you need to get used to monitoring it, particularly once your dog is an adult. Those snacks you share are not healthy, and your dog will pick up weight a lot faster than you will eating the same foods with less exercise. This is not really a reward for your Bulldog – it's a hazard. Keep your dog on a diet that is healthy instead of indulging the little cutie. This will keep you both a lot happier in the long run.

Counting calories is incredibly time consuming, but you should also know roughly how many calories your Bulldog eats in a day because it really does not take much to meet the needs of such a sedentary dog. It is also possible to weigh your Bulldog, though it will get very tricky as they get older. If you want to track your Bulldog's weight, ask your vet for the best way to weigh your adult Bulldog. This can help you keep your pooch happy and healthy.

Photo Courtesy of
Giianna Lagorio

CHAPTER 15
Grooming – Productive Bonding

Bulldogs have short hair that is fairly coarse, but they are moderate shedders for most of the year. However, with the constant petting and attention, your Bulldog's coat can actually feel fairly soft. The problem is the wrinkles. Your Bulldog's skin is going to need to be cleaned regularly to keep the wrinkles from becoming infected.

The rest of the grooming will be fairly easy, though you do need to make sure that you schedule regular baths, nail clippings, and other activities to keep your Bulldog comfortable and healthy. They are a fairly easy breed to groom. Coupled with the low exercise needs, Bulldogs are a pretty low-maintenance breed that can be highly entertaining. This is part of what makes them so easy to love.

Managing Your Bulldog's Coat – It's Easy

"Bath only as needed. Too much bathing can dry out their coats. Also, at times their noses may get pretty dry so I will put either Coconut Oil or Vitamin E oil on their noses."

Kym Thew
Bullyful Bulldogs

Bulldogs do need at least weekly brushing, though two or three times a week is recommended. This will help you to remember to check the folds between their wrinkles for signs of infection. It is also a great way to bond with your Bulldog, no matter what age he is. The regular attention will be something that your dog will look forward to as a part of the routine. It will also be a nice way to relieve stress as petting a dog is an easy way to help you calm down. Since Bulldogs will probably love the extra, regular attention, it isn't going to be much of a chore. This makes it a quick and easy task that everyone can enjoy.

Puppy

As you can probably guess, brushing a puppy is going to take you more time. There will be a lot of wiggling and attempts at play. Trying to tell your puppy that the brush is not a toy clearly isn't going to work, so be prepared to be patient during each brushing session. On the other hand, they are so adorable that you probably won't mind that it takes a bit longer.

You can plan to brush your puppy after playing so that your Bulldog has far less energy to fight or play. Be careful that you don't encourage rambunctious behavior during brushing because this will become part of

Photo Courtesy of Samantha Raney

the routine, and your Bulldog will think that the brushing is meant for playtime, making it difficult to convince him that it isn't true the longer the playing happens. Initially you might not mind, but there will be times when you just want to finish brushing your dog quickly, and that is why you need to make sure your puppy doesn't think it is time to play.

As you get accustomed to brushing your puppy, start checking your pup's skin. Look for rashes, sores, or infections. You should also check his eyes, ears, and mouth while you are grooming him. Keep doing these activities even after your Bulldog is an adult.

> **FUN FACT**
> **Celebrity Bulldogs**
>
> Gloria Estefan, Grammy Award-winning singer-song-writer and renowned philanthropist, is an activist for animal rescue and shelters. She owns a number of rescued pets and has authored a book series based on her bulldog, Noelle, beginning with the book The Magically Mysterious Adventures of Noelle the Bulldog.

Adulthood

Photo Courtesy of Kaila Valle

Tangles are not something you have to worry about with Bulldogs, but you do need to be careful of their skin. Brushing probably won't take too long, so brushing him two or three times a week isn't going to be a burden. You will definitely want to keep this schedule during the spring and fall when you notice that your canine is shedding a bit more often.

Baths should be a regular part of the schedule too, although it will vary based on the time of year. If you keep your Bulldog brushed a few times a week, baths can be once a month or two (depending on how much time you spend outside with your furry friend).

Skin Care

"Clean their wrinkles as often as they need. Some need daily cleaning and some only weekly. It will depend on the age of your Bulldog as well as the wrinkles your dog carries. Make sure to check the entire tail and base."

Sandra Fulton-Cooper
Bodanna Bulldogs

Another thing you need to clean regularly is the wrinkles on the face and body. You should have become used to checking these with your puppy, but now you are going to clean them regularly. The wrinkles can trap dirt, making them potentially dangerous little areas that can become infected. This is a really quick activity, but you do need to be careful. You can use a lightly damp cloth so that you don't make the folds of the wrinkles wet. Alternatively, Benjamin De Jesus of Champion Bullies suggests that you "clean folds and tail daily with baby wipes."

Given how much Bulldogs drool, you are definitely going to find dirt every time you clean them. If your dog accumulates dirt quickly, you may need to make this part of your daily routine.

In addition to cleaning the wrinkles on the face, you are going to need to make a habit of cleaning other wrinkles, such as around the middle and tail.

Sandra Fulton-Cooper of Bodanna Bulldogs sums up the wrinkle cleaning process well: "Clean wrinkles as often as they need. Some need daily cleaning and some only weekly. It will depend on the age of your Bulldog as well as the wrinkles your dog carries. Make sure to check the entire tail and base."

Photo Courtesy of Apryl King

Photo Courtesy of
Sam Cox

Trimming The Nails

You have to be very careful about trimming the nails, even though they have such big paws. If you feel at all uncomfortable, you might want to have a professional trim your Bulldog's nails. You can always study how it is done and learn how to do it yourself over time. While he is still a puppy though, your Bulldog may be a little too enthusiastic for you to do the cutting.

The puppy's nails should be cut about once a week since your Bulldog will probably be on concrete and asphalt less often than a larger dog. Without these hard surfaces to help keep the nails filed, regular grooming will be required to keep the nails from being too long.

Once your dog is an adult, check the nails monthly. Since you will be walking him more often on sidewalks or other kinds of hard surfaces that will help keep his nails shorter, grooming can be done less frequently. Since you won't be walking too much, you will need to plan to trim the nails about every other week.

Brushing Their Teeth

A Bulldog's teeth should be brushed at least a few times a week, although daily brushing is recommended because of the way your Bulldog's face is constructed. Regular brushing keeps the dog's teeth clean and healthy. If you notice that plaque and tartar are building up quickly, or that your dog's breath is smelling foul faster, you can increase how often you conduct the brushing ritual.

Cleaning Their Ears And Eyes

Just like every dog, you will need to be careful about cleaning their eyes and ears during bath time. In addition to cleaning wrinkles, you are going to need to make sure you don't get the ears or eyes wet when you are cleaning their faces.

CHAPTER 16
Health Issues

FUN FACT

**Bulldog
Health Research**

The Bulldog Club of America (BCA) sponsors research about health issues in bulldogs through its BCA Charitable Fund (BCACF). As of 2019, the BCACF has spent over $57,000 in grants for studies on conditions such as hypothyroid disease and pulmonic stenosis.

Bulldogs make exceptionally fantastic companions, in large part due to their absolute love of being close to you. Sadly their life expectancy is only 8 to 12 years, and you will need to take very good care of them. Overeating and overheating will be your primary concerns, but there are other potential health issues with the breed. One of the most unique issues is not a concern for most Bulldog owners, unless you intend to breed your Bulldog. It is best to avoid this if you have not bred the breed before because they have several significant breeding issues that make them a bad choice for new breeders. For example, Bulldog heads are too large for most mothers to birth the babies naturally.

As long as you are careful and take good care of your little buddy, you will still have many good years as your Bulldog puppy grows up and becomes an important part of your family. With such an uncanny ability to entertain and a desire to be a part of everything that happens in the family, your Bulldog may not let you know if something hurts. While it is one reason to make sure no one plays too rough with your Bulldog, it also means that they may not let you know if they have another type of problem – fleas or ticks.

In addition to making sure that your canine doesn't get overheated, there are some basic preventative measures you should take to make sure your puppy stays healthy. Many of the treatments and concerns are universal across the entire canine world, which means there is a good chance you already know how you need to take care of your dog. You can consider this chapter as more of a reminder or checklist of things you probably already know you need to be aware of. Treating and keeping your puppy free of parasites should be something that you add to your budget once they are old enough for the treatments.

Fleas And Ticks

Since Bulldogs don't require much outdoor time, they are at a lower risk of getting ticks. Fleas are something that you will need to watch for since fleas live in yards too. Your Bulldog is going to be outside some of the time, which means you still have to monitor him. If your Bulldog loves roaming through high grass, you cannot allow any lapse in treatment, even in winter.

With each bath that you give your Bulldog, you should make time to check for ticks and fleas as part of the cleaning process. You don't want to bathe your Bulldog too often, so if you check for fleas periodically, you will probably be all right (and as long as you keep up with the flea treatments). Comb through the fur and check the skin for irritation and parasites. This will help keep your puppy healthier and feeling much better. Since you will be doing this often, you should be able to know when a bump is a problem. Since your dog will be very happy to spend time with you, it shouldn't take as long as you think – it isn't as though you will have to spend a lot of time struggling to get your Bulldog to sit still for a tick check.

Photo Courtesy of
Nicandro Darpino

Photo Courtesy of
Christina Crawford

Fleas will be more problematic because they are far more mobile. The best way to look for fleas is to make it a regular part of your brushing sessions. You can also look for behavioral indicators, such as incessant scratching and licking. With the regular checks on your pup's skin when brushing his or her fur, you will be able to check the spots where your dog is scratching to see if the skin is irritated or if it is the work of a flea. Given how low to the ground Bulldogs tend to be, fleas will have no trouble jumping on your Bulldog from the grass or other vegetation. This means you will need to use flea preventative products on a regular basis. You won't be able to do this with puppies under a certain age, but once they mature, you can start adding treatment to the budget and schedule.

If you want to use natural products instead of the chemical-filled products, set aside a few hours to research the alternatives and find out what works best for your Bulldog. Because their skin is sensitive and should not be washed too often, increasing the frequency of baths should not be part of the solution. Do verify that any natural products work before you buy them.

Remedies should be applied monthly. Establishing a regular schedule and adding it to the calendar will help you remember to treat your dog on schedule.

Worms And Parasites

Although worms and other types of parasites are a less common problem than fleas and ticks, they can be far more dangerous. There are a number of types of worms that you should be aware of:

- Heartworms

- Hookworms

- Roundworms

- Tapeworms

- Whipworms

One of the primary problems is that there isn't an easy-to-recognize set of symptoms to help identify when your dog has a problem with worms. However, you can keep an eye out for these symptoms, and if your dog shows them, you should schedule a visit to the vet.

- If your Bulldog is unexpectedly lethargic for at least a few days.

- Patches of fur begin to fall out (this will be noticeable if you brush your Bulldog regularly) or if you notice patchy spaces in your dog's coat.

Photo Courtesy of
Pryscila Cordero

- If your dog's stomach becomes distended (expands), set up an appointment immediately to have him or her checked. Your dog's stomach will look like a potbelly.
- Your Bulldog begins coughing, vomiting, has diarrhea, or has a loss in appetite.

These symptoms should be more obvious in a Bulldog because they tend to be active or with you all the time. If you aren't sure, it is best to get to the vet as soon as possible to check.

If your dog has hookworms or roundworms, you will also need to visit a doctor to get checked. These worms can be spread to you from your dog through skin contact. If your dog has them, you are at risk of contracting them. Being treated at the same time can help stop the vicious cycle of continually switching which of you has worms.

Heartworms are a significant threat to your dog's health as they can be deadly. You should be actively treating your dog to ensure that this parasite does not have a home in your dog. There are medications that can ensure your Bulldog does not get or have heartworms.

Benefits Of Veterinarians

Your dog should have regular visits to your vet, just like you have regular checkups for yourself. From regular shots to healthy checkups, vets will make sure that your Bulldog stays healthy. With a number of potential issues, you want to make sure that your Bulldog doesn't have any of the many possible problems.

Since Bulldogs are such eager companions, it is going to be obvious when they aren't acting normal. Annual visits to the vet will ensure there isn't a problem that is slowly draining the energy or health from your dog.

Health checkups also make sure that your Bulldog is aging well. If there are any early symptoms of something potentially wrong with your dog over the years (such as arthritis), you will be able to start making adjustments. The vet can help you come up with ways to manage pain and problems that come with the aging process. Your vet will be able to recommend adjustments to the schedule to accommodate your canine's aging body and diminishing abilities. This will ensure that you can keep having fun together without hurting your dog. These changes are well worth it in the end because your dog will able to keep enjoying time with you without suffering additional pain.

Photo Courtesy of Christopher Liley

Holistic Alternatives

Wanting to keep a dog from a lot of exposure to chemical treatments makes sense, and there are many good reasons why people are moving to more holistic methods. However, doing this does require a lot more research and monitoring to ensure that the methods are working – and more importantly, do not harm your dog. Unverified holistic medicines can be a waste of money, or worse, they can even be harmful to your pet. Other methods have often been used for far longer, so there is more data to ensure that they aren't doing more harm than good. However, natural methods that work are always preferable to any chemical solution.

If you decide to go with holistic medication, talk with your vet about your options. You can also seek out Bulldog experts to see what they recommend before you start using any methods you are interested in trying. Read what scientists have said about the medicine. There is a chance that the products you buy from a store are actually better than some holistic medications.

Make sure you are thorough in your research and that you do not take any unnecessary risks with the health of your Bulldog.

Vaccinating Your Bulldog

Vaccination schedules are almost universal for all dog breeds, including Bulldogs. Use the following schedule to ensure that your Bulldog receives the shots needed on time.

- The first shots are required at between 6 and 8 weeks following the birth of your Bulldog. You should find out from the breeder if these shots have been taken care of and get the records of the shots:

    - Corona virus
    - Leptospirosis
    - Distemper
    - Parainfluenza
    - Hepatitis
    - Parvo

- These same shots are required again at between 10 and 12 weeks of age.

- These same shots are required again at between 14 and 15 weeks old, as well as his or her first rabies shot.

- Your dog will need to get these shots annually after that. Your Bulldog will also need annual rabies shots afterward.

Once you start the shots, you need to see them through to the end. Make sure to get the schedule for upkeep on these shots. Then you will need to maintain these shots over the years, particularly shots like rabies.

CHAPTER 17
Health Concerns

All purebred dogs have common health problems specific to their breed. You will need to monitor for those health problems as your Bulldog ages. Knowing what the potential problems are so that you can watch for them can help you know what to do and when to talk to your vet. The sooner you start to counter any potential problems, the longer your Bulldog is likely to live and the healthier he or she is likely to be. This means more time enjoying each other's company. If you notice any of the symptoms listed in the earlier chapters, make sure to schedule an appointment with your vet to have your dog checked.

Photo Courtesy of Clark Saltz

Adopting a puppy can give you the span of a dog's entire life to ensure your dog is as healthy as possible. The breeder should be able to provide health records in addition to any shot records and required tests. All of the details on the genetic and common ailments of Bulldog are in Chapter 4. Making sure that the parents are healthy increases the likelihood that your puppy will remain healthy into the golden years. However, there is still a chance that your dog will have one of these documented problems even if the parents don't. This is why you have to keep an eye on your furry friend.

Photo Courtesy of Laura Fritter

A Dog With A Lot Of Possible Health Concerns

Overall, the Bulldog is a fairly healthy breed. This may come as a surprise given their looks and the funny gait they have, but they don't have many genetic ailments.

There are two primary concerns that require your attention – your dog's face and their uniquely shaped bodies.

Face

The Bulldog's face is very distinctive. As you learn to smile at that little panting sound that follows you around the house, you should be aware that the noisiness of Bulldogs is also a sign of how difficult it is for them to breathe. Easily the most dangerous health problem your Bulldog will have is overheating. With the way their faces are shaped, Bulldogs have trouble breathing. It is entirely too easy for them to get too hot, and it can be fatal. Always be aware of how your Bulldog is feeling. When they start to overheat, their tongues will hang out further than normal and they will pant more heavily than normal. Check the tongue and if there is a bluish tint to it, your Bulldog is overheating. Providing your best friend with some ice and cold water can help to get your Bulldog's temperature down.

Some breeders will say that Bulldogs are a healthy breed. Others say that they aren't. This kind of inconsistency shows just how much of a variable genetics are.

The wrinkles are adorable, but also problematic. As covered in Chapter 15, grooming includes keeping the wrinkles clean.

Body

Photo Courtesy of Jacqueline Orincsak

The Bulldog's body looks incredibly sturdy, which tends to make people feel they can be rougher with their Bulldog. It's not true. Playing with Bulldogs is encouraged, but you always need to make sure that playtime does not include roughhousing.

While they don't have many genetic issues, some Bulldogs do have malformed spines and hips, which can cause them pain. Given the way their legs are bowed, it likely does not come as a surprise that they may have problems with their knees.

Another potential issues is gastric torsion. This is when a dog's stomach twists, which can cut off the blood supply. This condition is common in dogs with similar shapes, including Greyhounds, German Shepherds, and other dogs with chests that are considerably larger than the dog's waist.

Typical Pure-Breed Health Issues

Bulldogs don't tend to suffer from genetic issues as much as from their unique physical makeup. There are a number of potential problems, but most Bulldogs tend to be healthy. This means that there is low risk, but that doesn't mean no risk. Keep a careful eye on your Bulldog over the years so that you are more likely to notice any potential issues.

Where You Can Go Wrong

In addition to genetic problems, there are things that you can do that could damage your dog's health. These are related to the dog's diet and exercise levels. If you follow the recommendations in Chapter 16, your dog will remain healthy longer.

Importance Of Breeder To Ensuring Health In Your Bulldog

Being aware of the health of the parents and the diseases that are known to be a problem for them or their parents will help you know what to monitor for in your Bulldog.

Any breeder that doesn't provide a health guarantee for a breed as established as the Bulldog is not a breeder you should consider. Avoid all of these breeders – they are interested in the money, and the dog's health is of little to no concern to them. If a breeder says that a puppy or litter has to be kept in an isolated location for health reasons, do not work with that breeder.

Photo Courtesy of Julie Swenson

Ask the breeder to talk about the history of the parents, the kinds of health problems that have been in the dog's family, and if the breeder has had problems with any particular illness in the past. If the breeder gives you only short or vague answers, this is a sign that the breeder has dogs that are more likely to have issues later.

Common Diseases And Conditions

Bulldogs have problems with specific parts of their bodies a lot more often than most breeds. The following are the areas where you need to monitor your Bulldog:

Photo Courtesy of
Patrick & Mariah Hardesty

- Skin
- Breathing
- Tail
- Heart

- Patella
- Thyroid
- Knee problems

Prevention & Monitoring

Beyond genetic issues (something you should learn about the parents before getting your puppy), the problem you have to worry about is weight. Previous chapters provide information about the right diet and exercise for your Bulldog. Refraining from giving your Bulldog foods made of grains and keeping their daily caloric intake

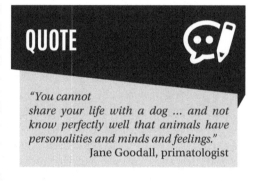

QUOTE

"You cannot share your life with a dog ... and not know perfectly well that animals have personalities and minds and feelings."
Jane Goodall, primatologist

within a healthy range area are essential given the dog's size. Considering the fact that they will eat whatever you give them, your dog's weight is always going to be a concern if you aren't careful. Your vet will likely talk to you if your dog has too much weight on its body because this not only puts a strain on the dog's legs, joints, and muscles, it can have adverse effects on your dog's heart, blood flow, and respiratory system.

CHAPTER 18
Your Aging Bulldog

"You never have a bad day when you have a Bulldog. They have the silliest personality and are always doing something goofy. They LOVE their people."

Sandra Fulton-Cooper
Bodanna Bulldogs

Bulldogs have a life expectancy of between 8 and 12 years. They are prone to some late in life problems, like hip dysplasia and knee problems, that will mean making some real changes in your life as your dog reaches the golden years. The senior Bulldog is between 7 and 8 years old and up. As your dog ages, you will need to start making adjustments to accommodate his or her reduced abilities. A dog may remain healthy his or her entire life, but the body just won't be able to do the same activities at 10 that it could do at 2. The changes you need to make will be based on your Bulldog's specific needs. The decline tends to be gradual, just little things here and there, like your Bulldog having less traction on smooth surfaces. Over time, the body will start to deteriorate so that your dog will not be able to jump as high.

As your Bulldog's energy and abilities decrease, you need to make sure that he or she is not overdoing it. You will need to be particularly careful with your dog and the temperature. Both hot and cold can be bad for senior Bulldogs.

HELPFUL TIP
Memorial Donations

When it's time to say goodbye to your aging dog, you may want to prolong the legacy of your beloved pet. Many animal rescue organizations and shelters gladly accept donations in the name of departed pets. Check with your local shelters for options in your area.

These later years will be just as much fun; you will just need to make sure your Bulldog isn't pushing the new limitations. It is easy to make the senior years incredibly enjoyable for your Bulldog and yourself by making the necessary adjustments that allow your dog to keep being active without overexertion.

Senior Dog Care

It is usually easier to take care of a senior dog than a young dog, and the Bulldog is no exception. Naps are just as exciting as walks. Sleeping beside you while you watch television or even if you nap with your dog is pretty much all it takes to make your Bulldog happy (though that was probably true when they were young too).

However, you must continue to be vigilant about diet and exercise. Now is not the time to let your Bulldog start to eat anything and everything or neglect to take your regular walks. A senior Bulldog cannot handle extra weight, so you must be careful to ensure he or she remains healthy with age.

Photo Courtesy of Kelley Genest

You may only need one short walk, then indoor play to make sure you older Bulldog gets enough exercise. Since your Bulldog should never take long walks, the exercise schedule may not change much. Still, you may find that those short walks are even shorter, with your Bulldog only being able to walk a couple of houses away from home. Don't try to push your Bulldog to go further. If your little furry friend can only walk a couple of houses down the sidewalk, that is fine. There are games you can play inside that won't hurt your Bulldog.

When it comes to items that your Bulldog will need to access regularly, you should make some changes to your current configuration.

- Set water bowls out in a couple of different places so that your dog can easily reach them as needed.

- Cover hard floor surfaces (such as tiles, hardwood, and vinyl). Use carpets or rugs that will not slip out from under your Bulldog.

- Add cushions and softer bedding for your Bulldog. This will both make the surface more comfortable and help your Bulldog stay warmer. There are some bed warmers for dogs if your Bulldog displays achy joints or muscles often. Of course, you also need to make sure your Bulldog isn't too warm, so this can be a fine balancing act.

- Increase how often you brush your Bulldog to improve his or her circulation. This should be very agreeable to your Bulldog as a way to make up for other limitations that mean you can do other activities less often.

- Stay inside in extreme heat and cold. Your Bulldog is hardy, but the old canine body cannot handle the extreme changes as well as once it did.

- Use stairs or ramps for your Bulldog instead of constantly picking up your canine. Picking your Bulldog up may be more convenient for you, but it is not healthy for you or your Bulldog. Let your dog maintain a bit more self-sufficiency.

- Avoid changing your furniture around, particularly if your Bulldog shows signs of having trouble with his or her sight. A familiar home is more comforting and less stressful as your pet ages. If your Bulldog is not able to see as clearly as he or she once did, keeping the home familiar will make it easier for your dog to move around without getting hurt.

- If you have stairs, consider setting up an area where your dog can stay without having to use the stairs as often.

- Create a space where your Bulldog can relax with fewer distractions and noises. Your Bulldog will probably be even less comfortable being left alone for extended periods, but you should have a place where you and your older dog can just relax without loud or startling noises. Don't make your little friend feel isolated, but do give him or her a place to get away from everyone if he needs to be alone.

- Be prepared to let your dog out more often for restroom breaks.

Nutrition

Since a decrease in exercise is inevitable for any aging dog (even the largely lounging Bulldog), you will need to adjust your pet's diet. If you opt to feed your Bulldog commercial dog food, make sure you change to the senior food. If you make your Bulldog's food, take the time to research how best to reduce calories without sacrificing taste. Your canine is going to need less fat in his or her food, so you may need to find something healthier that still has a lot taste to supplement the types of foods you gave your Bulldog as a puppy or active adult dog.

Exercise

"A Bulldog does not need much exercise. If you do walk your Bulldog, be sure to do it either early in the morning or later in the evening to avoid the heat of the day. Bulldogs are very prone to overheating if they over exert in hot weather. There are plenty of ways for your Bulldog to get exercise indoors as well. Playing tug with a rope or throwing ball."

Kym Thew
Bullyful Bulldogs

Exercise will be entirely up to you because your Bulldog is still just happy to be with you. If you make fewer demands, decrease the number of walks, or in any way change the routine, your Bulldog will quickly adapt to the new program. It is up to you to adjust the schedule and keep your Bulldog comfortable with the activities you do together. You may get to the point where you only go out with your Bulldog for restroom breaks and the occasional walk around the immediate area. Your Bulldog is probably going to be perfectly fine with that as long as there is enough indoor playtime.

Keep in mind that your Bulldog is more likely to gain weight in the later years, something that his or her body really cannot handle. While the exercise will be reduced, it should not be eliminated. Keep to what your dog can manage and adjust his food accordingly to keep the weight healthy.

This will probably be the hardest part of watching your Bulldog age. However, you will need to watch your Bulldog for signs of tiredness or pain so that you can stop exercising before your dog has done too much. Your pace will need to be slower and your attention more on your dog, but ultimately it can be just as exciting. You will probably notice that your Bulldog spends more time sniffing. This could be a sign that your dog is tiring, or it could be his or her way of acknowledging that long steady walks are a thing of the past and is stopping to enjoy the little things more. It is an interesting time and gives you a chance to get to understand your Bulldog as the years start to show. Your Bulldog may also let you know that it is time to go home by turning around to go back or sitting down a lot and looking at you. Take the hint and go home if your Bulldog lets you know that the limits have been reached.

Photo Courtesy of
Sonia Barajas

Mental Stimulation

Unlike the body, your Bulldog's mind is usually going to be just as sharp and clever in the golden years. That means you can start making adjustments to focus more on the activities that are mentally stimulating. Games like hide and seek or puzzles will be right up your Bulldog's alley. You can start doing training for fun because your Bulldog will be just as able to learn now as when he or she was one year old. Actually, it is likely to be easier because your Bulldog has learned to focus better and the bond will make him happy to have something he can still do with you.

Your Bulldog will be grateful for the shift in focus and additional attention. Getting your senior Bulldog new toys is one way to help keep your dog's mind active if you do not want to train your dog or if you just don't have the time. Do be careful about chew toys though as your Bulldog's teeth will not be nearly as firm as they once were. You can then teach the Bulldog different names for the toys because it will be fascinating (after all, he or she will still work for praise). Whatever toys you get, make sure they are not too rough on your dog's older jaws and teeth. Tug of war may be a game of the past (you don't want to hurt the old teeth), but other games are still very much appreciated.

Hide and seek is another game that your aging Bulldog can manage with relative ease. Whether you hide toys or yourself, this can be a game that keeps your Bulldog guessing.

Regular Vet Exams

Just as humans go to visit the doctor more often as they age, you are going to need to take your dog to see your vet with greater frequency. The vet can make sure that your Bulldog is staying active without being too active, and that there is no unnecessary stress on your older dog. If your canine has sustained an injury and hidden it from you, your vet is more likely to detect it.

Your vet can also make recommendations about activities and changes to your schedule based on your Bulldog's physical abilities and any changes in personality. For example, if your Bulldog is panting more now, it could be a sign of pain from stiffness. This could be difficult to distinguish given how much Bulldogs pant as a rule, but if you see other signs of pain, schedule a visit with the vet. Your vet can help you determine the best way to keep your Bulldog happy and active during the later years.

157

Photo Courtesy of Laurie Sangster

Common Old-Age Ailments

Chapters 4 and 17 cover the illnesses that are common or likely with a Bulldog, but old age tends to bring a slew of ailments that are not particular to any one breed. Here are the things you will need to watch for (as well as talking to your vet about them).

- Diabetes is probably the greatest concern for a breed that loves to eat as much as your Bulldog does, especially because he probably isn't going to get much exercise. Although it is usually thought of as a genetic condition, any Bulldog can become diabetic if not fed and exercised properly. It is another reason why it is so important to be careful with your Bulldog's diet and exercise levels.

- Arthritis is probably the most common ailment in any dog breed, and the Bulldog is no exception. If your dog is showing signs of stiffness and pain after normal activities, it is very likely that he or she has arthritis. Talk with your vet about safe ways to help minimize the pain and discomfort of this common joint ailment.

- Gum disease is a common issue in older dogs as well, and you should be just as vigilant about brushing teeth when your dog gets older as you do at any other age. A regular check on your Bulldog's teeth and gums can help ensure this is not a problem.

- Loss of eyesight or blindness is relatively common in older dogs, just as it is in humans. Unlike humans, however, dogs don't do well with wearing glasses. Have your dog's vision checked at least once a year and more often if it is obvious that his or her eyesight is failing. Those large eyes will need extra attention.

- Kidney disease is a common problem in older dogs, and one that you should monitor for the older your Bulldog gets. If your canine is drinking more often and having accidents regularly, this could be a sign of something more serious than just aging. If you notice this happening, get your Bulldog to the vet as soon as possible and have him or her checked for kidney disease.

Enjoying The Final Years

The last years of your Bulldog's life can actually be just as enjoyable (if not more so) than earlier stages. The energy and the activities that the two of you used to do will be replaced with more attention and relaxation than at any other time. Finally having your Bulldog be calm enough to just sit still

Photo Courtesy of Ashtan Hill

and enjoy your company can be incredibly nice (just remember to keep up his or her activity levels instead of getting too complacent with your Bulldog's love of resting and relaxing).

Steps And Ramps

Bulldogs are not exactly a size that makes them easy to lift. Picking up your dog more often as they age can even do more physical harm. There are two good reasons to ensure your Bulldog is able to move around without you picking him or her up.

- Having an older body means they are fragile and should not be picked up to help them avoid unnecessary pain.

- Independence in movement is best for you and your Bulldog. You do not want your Bulldog to come to expect you to pick him or her up every time he or she wants to get on the furniture or into the car.

Steps and ramps are the best way to ensure your Bulldog can keep some level of self-sufficiency. Also, you don't want to spoil your Bulldog in the later years. Using steps and ramps provides a bit of different activity that can work as a way of getting a bit of extra exercise.

Enjoy The Advantages

A Bulldog can be just as much fun in old age because his or her favorite thing is being with you. Your pet is just as mischievous as during the early years, but has learned to chill a bit more.

Your pet will find the warmest and most comfortable places, and will want you to join him or her. Your dog is incredibly devoted and will be happy to just share a short stroll followed by a lazy evening at home.

What To Expect

Your Bulldog probably isn't going to suffer from fear that you are less interested in spending time together. He or she will continue be the loving mischief maker at every opportunity – that does not change with age. Just how much they can do changes. Your canine's limitations should dictate interactions and activities. If you are busy, make sure you schedule time with your Bulldog to do things that are within those limitations. Your happiness is still of utmost importance to your dog, so let the dear old canine know you feel the same way about his or her happiness. It is just as easy to make an older Bulldog happy as it is with a young one, and it is easier on you since relaxing is more essential.

Made in the USA
Las Vegas, NV
05 December 2021

36125514R00090